*A Voyage at Sea
with Don Quixote*

*A Voyage at Sea with Don Quixote*

Thomas Mann

Translated by John Broadwin

ALMA CLASSICS

ALMA CLASSICS
an imprint of

ALMA BOOKS LTD
60 High Street
Wimbledon Village
London SW19 5EE
United Kingdom
www.almaclassics.com

Represented by:
Authorised Rep Compliance Ltd
Ground Floor
71 Lower Baggot Street
Dublin, D02 P593
Ireland
www.arccompliance.com

A Voyage at Sea with Don Quixote first published in German in 1934 as *Meerfahrt mit Don Quijote*
This edition first published by Alma Classics in 2026

Cover: David Wardle

Translation and Notes © John Broadwin, 2026

Printed in Great Britain by CPI Group (UK) Ltd, Croydon CR0 4YY

ISBN: 978-1-84749-936-3

All rights reserved. No part of this publication may be reproduced, stored in or introduced into a retrieval system, or transmitted, in any form or by any means (electronic, mechanical, photocopying, recording or otherwise), without the prior written permission of the publisher. This book is sold subject to the condition that it shall not be resold, lent, hired out or otherwise circulated without the express prior consent of the publisher.

Contents

A Voyage at Sea with Don Quixote	1
19th May 1934	5
20th May	15
21st May	27
22nd May	37
23rd May	45
24th May	53
26th May	69
27th May	79
28th May	87
Notes	97
Extra Material	105

*A Voyage at Sea
with Don Quixote*

TRANSLATOR'S DEDICATION

IN MEMORIAM
My parents Bertyl Berlin 1915–2008 and Henry Broadwin 1913–53
My maternal grandparents Leo 1877–1968 and Elsie Muller 1889–1980
My paternal grandparents Emma 1888–1964 and Morris Brodowsky 1880–1954
My maternal uncle Dr George H. Muller 1919–2011
My stepfather Ernst Berlin 1906–87

19th May 1934

We thought the first thing we would do is have a vermouth in the bar, and that is what we are doing now, while quietly waiting for the ship to depart. I had taken from my travel bag this notebook and one of the four little orange cloth-bound volumes of *Don Quixote*, my travelling companion on this voyage – there was no rush to unpack anything else. After all, we have nine to ten days until we land in the Antipodes, the opposite side of the earth, and by the time Saturday and Sunday roll around again and Monday and Tuesday have been added, this civilized adventure will have come to an end – the easygoing Dutch vessel, whose gangway we walked up a short while ago, will not reach its destination any faster. And why should it? Its speed is in keeping with its comfortable medium size and is more natural and saner than the breakneck pace of those colossi racing over the expanse that lies before us as they try to set a record of six or even four days to make the crossing. Take it easy, slow down – andante! Richard Wagner claimed that the andante was the true German tempo. But partial answers such as his to the perennial question "What is German?" are arbitrary and counterproductive, incentivizing the denigration of any number of things as "un-German" that are anything but, for example the allegretto, the scherzando and the spiritoso.

Wagner's remark would have been more acceptable if he had omitted the reference to nationality and ethnicity, "sentimentalizing" and romanticizing it, and had limited himself to the objective value that I, like him, ascribe to the quality of slowness. All good things take time. And so do great things – or, to put it another way, space needs its time. I have often felt there is a kind of hubris, something sacrilegious, in robbing or depriving space of a dimension, of its natural connection to time. Goethe, clearly a friend of humankind, did not like microscopes and telescopes, because he felt that they artificially increased a human being's natural power to perceive reality, confusing the unaided human senses, and I am sure he would have approved of my misgivings, which raises the question where does sacrilege begin and where does it end, and whether ten days are as harmful as six or four. To be fair, an equal number of weeks should be set aside to give the ocean a rest, and we should use the power of the wind, a natural source of energy – like steam power. Of course, we do use fuel oil to heat the water. All this speculation is starting to look like a flight of fancy.

There is an explanation, though. It is a sign of my inner excitement. Put simply, I have stage fright – and is it any wonder? I am about to embark on my maiden voyage across the Atlantic, have my first encounter and make my first acquaintance with one of the world's great oceans – and, at the end of the trip, on the other side of the earth's curvature, over which waves of this gigantic body of water roll, New Amsterdam,* the world's quintessential megacity, is awaiting us. There are only four or five such cities in the world, and they are unique, monstrous in size and extravagant in design, standing out even among those cities we call metropolises, just as in nature elemental features of the landscape, such as deserts, mountains and seas, are in a class by themselves. I grew up on the shores of the Baltic, a provincial body of water, and in my blood are the traditions of an ancient midsize city, civilized and gentle, which endows its inhabitants with a sensitive imagination that views the elemental forces of nature with a sense of awe – and a sense of irony, to deflate them. I am reminded of the time the Russian writer Ivan Goncharov was travelling on the high seas* and a ferocious storm sprang up. The ship's captain went down to his cabin and asked him to come on deck. "You're a writer," the captain said. "You've got to see this, it's awesome." When the author of *Oblomov* came on deck, he looked around and said, "Yes, it's quite a nuisance, isn't it?" – and went back below.

It is reassuring to know that we will confront this vast, untamed ocean within the confines of civilization and under its care, while sailing on a sturdy vessel whose promenade decks, varnished cabin passageways, lounges and carpeted staircases we have just briefly inspected and whose brave officers and crew have been specially trained to deal with the power of nature. Like the luxurious Khartoum Express, with its radiant white cars and deep-blue glass windows, which carries travellers to the capital of the Sudan through a horrific wasteland interspersed with the blazing, death-threatening hills of the Libyan and Arabian deserts, the ship will get us to our destination... "exposed" – the very word makes you realize what it means to feel secure within the bounds of human civilization. I have little respect for those who face the elemental powers of nature and praise its "greatness" in lyric poetry without also accepting its chilling, unfeeling hostility.

The season we are in lessens some of the stresses associated with this adventure and mitigates nature's hostility. We are well into spring, and expect that from now on the ocean is not likely to play any tricks on us and that our sea legs will be up to any reasonable demands made on them, not least because we have filled our travel bags with a supply of Vasano seasickness tablets, yet another example of the resources provided by human civilization. How different it would be if it were winter! Friends of mine, artists on concert tour, have told me about the absurdities and horrors they experienced during a winter crossing, which I am sure I will not be spared some day. Waves? They're mountains, Everests! So we're not allowed on deck at the moment. Goncharov, that irascible Russian, would never have been brought up from his cabin if he had been on our ship now. Anyway, you can see the ocean better through a securely bolted porthole. In your cabin you hold on to your bedframe and bob up and down – it's like being tormented by one of those roller-coasters in a so-called amusement park as it tumbles your belly and your head this way and that. From a dizzying height you see your washstand careening towards you and your trunks bumping into each other in a clumsy dance on the sloping, shifting floor. There is a hideous, infernal din, caused by the violent weather raging outside and the ship punching its way forward, making every nut and bolt rattle and lasting for three days and four nights. Imagine you have two such days behind you and you have to contend with a third. And you haven't had a bite to eat. Then the moment comes when you are forced to recall your old habits. And because you haven't died, even though for any number of hours you were ready to call it quits, you are forced at some point to start eating again, and you ring for the steward because the electric bell still works and the ship's first-class hotel service still functions: even as the world is falling apart, the staff remains professional to the end – another example of civilization's refined and admirable heroism. The waiter arrives, wearing a white jacket, a towel draped over his arm – he doesn't fall into the cabin, but stands erect in the doorway. In the midst of this bedlam, he manages to hear your barely audible order, goes and comes back, carrying covered dishes that he balances precariously on his supple arms. He waits for a moment – a specific moment – when the state of the universe will allow him to swing the dishes along a trajectory that he can calculate but not control, and land them on your bed. Seeing that moment, he seizes it, acts with resolve and skill, and lets them fly. It looks as if the dishes are on course. But in that same moment the state of the universe has changed, and you discover the dishes lying upside down on your wife's bed. Incredible...

These are some of my stories, and they come to mind while we are sipping our farewell vermouth and I am jotting down these lines. And why shouldn't I? I don't need to enhance the respect I have for our undertaking, because I am respectful by nature, and like all who are endowed with the gift of imagination, provincial as it is entertaining, I go through life with my eyebrows lifted. With imagination, you will never become an elitist, because it "saves" you – if that is the proper word – from feeling superior to others. To be imaginative does not mean to dream things up: rather, it means to create something out of what already exists – and that is hardly elitist. We are now retracing Columbus's westward route – for days we will be floating in the cosmic space between two continents, while enjoying first-class service. I am sure the majority of our fellow passengers don't give a thought to the nature of our voyage and certainly not to that thought. And where are they, anyway? We are alone in this spacious bar, with its fine leather stools and sofas, its cosy, relaxing atmosphere. It suddenly occurs to me that we were also as good as alone on the tender that took us from the Boulogne-Maritime Station across the harbour water to our ship. Overhearing us, the bar steward comes over and, shaking his head, tells us that four passengers in first class, including us, boarded in Boulogne, that about a dozen came from Rotterdam, and four more would be embarking at Southampton. "That's it," he said. "What do you think?" he asked. What we think is that the cruise line is going to lose a lot of money on this trip. It's so sad, he said, what with the crisis, the "Depression". Even so, we all agreed that when the ship reverses direction and heads east, things will look up. The season for American tourists to visit Europe begins in June: Salzburg, Bayreuth and Oberammergau will beckon them to come over. "And there will be plenty," he said – by which he meant plenty of tips. Though he is still worried, this poor, distressed soul seems relatively happy – given the prospect of those rich pickings. We for our part think about how nice it will be to travel on a nearly empty ship. Being almost alone, we will have it practically to ourselves: it will be like living on a private yacht. The thought of all that peace and quiet brings me back to my shipboard reading, the little volume bound in orange cloth that is lying beside me – the other three parts of the set are in my cabin.

Shipboard reading – the term itself implies lowbrow fare. There is a widespread belief that vacation reading has to be intellectually unchallenging – trash "to pass one's idle hours". That is something I have never understood. Apart from the fact that "light reading" is the most boring in the world, it is beyond me why, on a special occasion such as a voyage, which is as serious as it is festive, a person should lower his or her intellectual standards and read such nonsense. Do travel and the idea of getting away from it all create a psychological condition in which such silliness is less rebarbative than usual? Earlier, I spoke of respect. Because I respect this undertaking of ours, it is only proper that I respect the reading matter that accompanies it. And because *Don Quixote* is one of the great classics of world literature, it is perfectly suited for a journey that will take us halfway around the world. Writing it was a bold adventure, and reading it, though passive, is also an adventure, and well suited to this life at sea. Surprisingly, I have never read it through, from beginning to end. But I will do so now aboard ship and finish this labyrinth of tales in the ten days it will take us to cross the Atlantic.

The windlass creaked as I wrote down my resolution. We are under way. We go on deck, look back and then turn our gaze to the sea.

20th May

I should not be doing what I am doing now: sitting hunched over to write. It is not good for your health, because the sea, as the Americans who dine with us say, is "a little rough" and the liner's motions, though quiet and steady, are most noticeable on the upper deck, where the writing room is. It is also not a good idea to look through the window, because the bobbing up and down of the horizon has a negative effect on the mind, familiar in a way from earlier experiences, but forgotten until now. It is also not the best idea to look down on a sheet of paper and what is scribbled on it. But it is not easy, even in the most difficult circumstances, to break the habits of a lifetime, like sitting down to write only after taking a morning stroll and eating breakfast.

Last night, we stopped for a short while in Southampton to take on the few passengers who were scheduled to board at this last stop on the long voyage across the Atlantic. We covered a considerable distance in the night. The south coast of England is still visible, but not for long. Under an overcast grey sky, the equally grey, foam-flecked surface of the sea is completely empty. I have long felt that the sea as experienced aboard ship – where there is neither time nor space to experience the true completion of the circle it offers – cannot compare with the impression it makes when seen from the beach. I miss the thrill of seeing the waves crashing against the ground I'm standing on. The sea has been divested of its magic and charm, reduced to a highway, a shipping lane, and has lost its character as a panorama, a dream, an idea, a glimpse of eternity, and has become a setting. And that setting, it seems, is not aesthetically pleasing, but rather the opposite. Schopenhauer says: "It is beautiful of course to *see* things, but it is not at all beautiful to *be* them."* The truth of his aphorism, directed against wishful thinking, applies well to my experience of the sea. And getting comfortable with an illusion does not make it any better – even when doing so is made easier by the shameful number of conveniences and amenities available on an ocean-going liner.

There are always some unwelcome demands made on you at sea. During the first few hours there is the inevitable shock of exchanging solid ground for a ship's swaying deck. For days there is something unreal about walking down an undulating staircase that is rising and falling beneath you: you hold your spinning, protesting head, hoping it is just a bad joke. A crazy walk on deck this morning – often holding on for dear life and reeling forward like a drunk, shaking your head in contemptuous laughter because, strangely enough, even though it has nothing to do with your situation, you feel like blaming yourself for a condition that ends in such an undignified way – just as you blame your feet for being "heavy" when walking up a steep incline. I am happy to report that none of the discomforts I experienced aboard ship – neither hyperacidity nor shocks to the nervous system – diminish my love of the sea, a love that is in the blood of my family and has endured from earliest childhood. Being "indisposed" at sea is no reason to sulk. Seasickness leaves the mind intact, and often the appetite too. I have no grudge, so to speak, against the sea. And I wish the practitioners of natural cures well if they choose to dilute its water to make their concoctions.

> You wild friend of my youth,
> Once more we're joined together!

I recalled this morning a poem that Tonio Kröger addressed to the sea but could not finish,* because his heart was throbbing...

One of the symptoms of mild seasickness is drowsiness, even an abnormal need for sleep during the first few days. A change in air pressure may be to blame, but more likely it is the ship's constant swaying from side to side that lulls you to sleep, almost in the way an anaesthetic does. The underlying principle is doubtless the same as that applied to rocking a child to sleep, altering the brain's natural rhythm – a practice that was invented ages ago by nursemaids and wet nurses, though it is not always safe, like the gifts of the poppy.

Yesterday afternoon and evening I read a good deal of *Don Quixote*, to the accompaniment of music in the Blue Salon, and today I am going to continue reading it in my deckchair, an inferior version of Hans Castorp's splendid lounge chair in *The Magic Mountain*.* What a unique monument this book is! Although it is subject to the tastes of the time, more so than might be expected in a satire directed against those tastes, and more often than not includes obsequious professions of loyalty to the Crown, it rises above its time and displays a poetic sensibility that is uninhibited, nuanced and humane. Tieck's translation* in the lively and polished German of the Classical-Romantic period, when our language was at its height of perfection, delights me more than I can say, and is ideally suited to the book's grand comic style, tempting me once again to see the comic mode as the essence of the novel and the novel and the comic mode as one and the same, even though equating the one with the other probably cannot be substantiated objectively. The novel begins with a stylistic trick, combining the Romantic and comic modes to pass off the whole "famous and remarkable history" as a translation of an Arabic manuscript, along with a commentary written by a "Moor" – that is, the Arab historian Cide Hamete Benengeli, which the author then uses as window dressing for his narrative, often switching into indirect speech and exploiting phrases such as "the history recounts" or "Blessed be Allah!", which Benengeli repeats three times at the beginning of Chapter VIII in the second part, before continuing his observations. The summary chapter headings are wonderfully humorous, for example, the tongue-in-cheek tone of "Concerning the clever and amusing talk that passed between Sancho Panza and his wife, Teresa Panza, and other events worthy of happy memory", or the parodic-comic turn in "Regarding the matters that Benengeli says will be known to the reader if he reads with attention". Humour is best exemplified by Cervantes's portrayal of the two main characters and their multifaceted, ever-changing, deeply human relationship, something the author took special pride in when he compared his depiction of them with that in the appalling, plagiarized sequel.* The sequel, written by an unscrupulous incompetent who had been tempted by the prospect of cashing in on the novel's widespread popularity, motivated Cervantes to write the second part – though, as Goethe says, he had exhausted all the book's themes in the first part. The bogus sequel portrayed Don Quixote as nothing more than a figure of ridicule who deserves to be beaten up, and Sancho Panza as merely a glutton. In more than one passage in the second part, Cervantes defends his own work while condemning the sequel's simplified version of events, and in the prologue he engages in a polemic directed against the sequel in a tone that is a model of decorum and moderation – though only superficially. It needs a rhetorical device, so he can shift blame onto the reader for demanding revenge while depicting himself in a dignified manner worthy of his hero, the man of La Mancha. "You would like me to call him (the author of the false *Don Quixote*) an ass, a fool, an insolent dolt, but the thought has not even entered my mind: let his sin be his punishment, and let that be an end to it." How very Christian and high-minded! What Cervantes does object to is that "that man" called him old and a cripple – as if it had been in his (the author's) power "to stop time and halt its passage, or as if I had been wounded in some tavern and not at the greatest event ever seen" – by which he meant the Battle of Lepanto.* "And it should be noted," he countered wittily, "that one writes not with grey hair, but with the understanding, which greatly improves with age." All fine and good. But the mellowness that comes with age and grey hair proves ineffective in dealing with the false

Don Quixote's coarse and offensive stories, so Cervantes asks the reader to retell them to "that man" and show the incompetent scribbler "what temptations of the Devil are, one of the greatest of which is to give a man the idea that he can compose and publish a book and thereby win fame and fortune" – and that his stories reflect vengefulness, rage, murderous hate and the self-conscious anguish of an artist who realizes that something that is successful, apart from the fact that it is good, can be conflated with something that is successful because it is bad.

Cervantes had seen how a shoddy piece of work claiming to be the sequel to his book "had travelled the world" and been devoured with the same relish as the original. The false *Don Quixote* copied his book's crude but more popular burlesque elements: the fun of beating up a figure of ridicule, the gluttony that was expected of peasants. But that was all it had to offer. It had none of the original's warmth, inventive use of language or its melancholy and depth of feeling for the human condition. Sad to say, the public did not miss those qualities. Apparently, it saw no difference between the original and the plagiarized version. Nothing is more humiliating for a writer than that – so when Cervantes talks about the "loathing and disgust" caused by another *Don Quixote*, he's alluding to his own feelings, even though he ascribes them to the public, and when he says he had to write the second part of his book to rid his readers of them, he did so to purge himself. And those feelings stemmed not only from his reaction to the inferior imitation of his *Don Quixote*, but also from the success of his own book. The second part of *Don Quixote* was calculated to remind the reader that it was "cut by the same artisan and from the same cloth as the first" and was meant to restore the success of the first and salvage its ruined reputation as a successful literary art form. The second part no longer has the initial verve and light-hearted playfulness of its predecessor, and shows how, by chance or by choice, a book that began as a modest idea, a rollicking satire filled with hilarity, which the author conceived as a parody, turned into a book that deals not only with the life and traditions of a people, but also with humanity as a whole. If the ambition to achieve distinction had not played an important part in writing the second part, it would not have been weighted down with humanism, elements of high culture and an air of literary hauteur. The author works hard to bring out as clearly and forcefully as possible the complexity of the main characters, and tries, more than anything else, to be "the same artisan and from the same cloth as the first". We know Don Quixote is mad – his chivalric hallucinations are proof enough of that – yet his quirky, anachronistic behaviour is so noble, so pure of heart and decent, and his bearing so aristocratic, that laughter at his "doleful", bizarre mannerisms, physical and otherwise, is mingled with an astounding degree of respect, so that all who encounter him shake their heads and feel drawn to this pathetic yet magnificent figure, mad in one sense but otherwise a perfect nobleman. It is the human spirit, in the form of his eccentric behaviour, that sustains and ennobles Quixote and allows him to emerge from every humiliating experience with his moral dignity intact – and the fact that Sancho Panza, the pot-bellied glutton, with his proverbs, his mother wit and his peasant's common sense telling him to reject a mad "idea" that will only result in severe beatings and to instead favour the wineskin, still has a profound appreciation of the human spirit and is deeply attached to his master despite all the hardships his service entails, never abandoning him and remaining a faithful squire, even though he is occasionally forced to lie to his master, is absolutely wonderful, making even him loveable and endowing the figure in the novel with genuine humanity, lifting it from the sphere of the merely comic into the realm of heartfelt humour.

Sancho exemplifies the ordinary Spaniard and symbolizes the Spanish people's relationship to the noble madness of the knight errant whom, for better or for worse, he has been summoned to serve. I have been thinking about this since yesterday. Here you have a country that blithely turns a travesty of its national virtues – nobility, idealism, uncommon magnanimity and unselfish chivalry – into a symbol of national pride and wistfully and proudly sees itself reflected in its pages. Is it not strange? Spain passed the zenith of its power centuries ago and is now struggling to adapt to modernity. But what interests me is not the "grand sweep of history", but rather the story of individual human beings, their thoughts and emotions. Good-humoured self-mockery, freedom and an easygoing, artistically leavened relationship with itself do not guarantee that a people will have a prominent place in history, but they do give it charm – and, in the end, charm and its opposite also have a role to play in history. Regardless of what pessimistic historians say, human beings have a conscience, even if only an aesthetic one that tells them what is in good taste and what is in bad taste. And though they worship success and the achievements of the powerful, even if that success is initiated by a crime,* they don't forget the dark side of human nature, the wanton violence and brutality that take place in their midst, and they ultimately reject success based on power and the efficient use of force. History is the common reality we spring from, that we are part of, in which we have to prove ourselves, and where Don Quixote's anachronistic gallantry fails him. His story endears him to us and makes us laugh. But what would an anti-Don Quixote be like, a pessimistic Don Quixote who mocks ideals, a sinister Don Quixote who believes in violence, a brutal Don Quixote but still a Don Quixote? For all his melancholic humour, Cervantes never went that far.

21st May

*(Deckchair, promenade deck,
warm blanket and coat)*

The foghorn has been blaring almost incessantly since yesterday evening. Come to think of it, it went on continuously all night long, and this morning it started to warn ships again. It is raining a little; the horizon, our daily glimpse of infinity, is shrouded in grey, and our pace has slowed. It is windy, but the sea is still calm, so I will not dwell on the weather.

There was a notice in English this morning, posted on the bulletin board at the bottom of the stairs leading to the dining room, ordering passengers to assemble, with their tickets, at numbered lifeboat stations for instructions from an officer who was assigned to a designated boat to tell them what to do in an emergency. I did not notice others obeying the order, but even so, after finishing the bouillon served at this time by white-jacketed stewards, we headed for our rendezvous. I was intrigued by the idea of dealing with an emergency in a setting whose luxurious accommodations and amenities were designed to make passengers forget how dangerous life at sea can be. As we went, not sure exactly where we were supposed to go, we bumped into the chief steward, whom we knew from the dining room and who told us that he was the officer in charge of our boat as well as our instructor and guardian angel. He is a jovial Dutchman who speaks English and German, both with the same humorous lack of proficiency, easygoing and good-natured on the surface, but calculating and shifty underneath, clean-shaven, with gold-rimmed glasses resting on a thin, aquiline nose – the kind of nose you are most likely to see in Germany among the Swabians – and wearing a beautiful braided coat, hip-length but cut low and wide in the evening, like a dinner jacket. He takes us to where we are to meet the other passengers, a spot on the promenade deck, and in his quaint and amusing Dutch version of German, with its harsh, guttural sounds, he explains in an easygoing, matter-of-fact way how a lifeboat is launched – nothing could be simpler or more dependable, he says, it's motor-driven, well constructed, though a bit small when the waves are high – you can see it being lowered from the upper deck where it's suspended below the top of the balcony railing. We get in, and as it touches the water, he says, "I can take you home now."

Home. What a funny way to put it. It sounds as if all we have to do is give him our address while we are riding the waves and he will take us there in a lifeboat. Home – what does that mean, anyway? Does it mean Küsnacht near Zürich in Switzerland* – where I have been living for a year and feel more like a guest than at home – which I do not consider a proper destination for a lifeboat? Looking back in time, I wonder if it means my home in Munich's Herzogpark neighbourhood near the banks of the Isar, where I had expected to end my days, but which turned out to be a temporary lodging, a pied-à-terre? Home… I would have to go still further back, to the place of my childhood, to my parents' house in Lübeck, still standing but slipping ever deeper into the past. What a strange lifeboat coxswain and guardian angel you are, with your glasses, those gold triangles on your sleeves, and your "I can take you home now" – even though you have no idea where that is!

Well, at least we have been instructed what do in an emergency. We chatted a little with our angel. I wanted to know if he had ever been in an emergency himself and had helped to launch a lifeboat. "Three times," he said. "I've helped three times in my career to evacuate passengers – it's hard not to be involved in an emergency evacuation when you've been at sea as long as I have." "Why?" I asked. "Why did you have to evacuate them?" "Why, you run into something," he said in mock surprise. "What else? It's unavoidable when you're at sea for as long as we are." It was hard for us to imagine or picture how professionals, formally trained in the arts of navigation, whom we blindly put our trust in, could so easily and so often fail to live up to their promise and might at any moment run into something. We could not get anything more specific from him, because he was continually cracking jokes and had such a limited vocabulary. Anyway, maybe everything he had told us was just a lot of hot air, like "I can take you home now".

In the dining room our steward caters to an American family that apparently has unlimited resources and regularly requests items not on the menu, feasting themselves on lobster, champagne, caviar and baked Alaska.* He goes from table to table, his hands behind his back, a big professional smile behind his glasses, and favours each with a bit of his joviality. He spends an unusually long time at the Americans' table to make sure they get their special requests promptly, and even pokes his head into the kitchen. Being on a cruise ship allows you to reflect on such displays of wealth with a degree of detachment, because everyone here is well off. The meals are lavish, and an extremely popular feature of the line's service – and you can eat as much as you want. There are no fixed menus. You get a new sheet every day filled with a variety of choices and can put together any meal you like. If you wanted, you could eat all the different courses of a full-course meal every day, from the starters to the "ice creams". There are limits, of course, to what a person can eat. And the line's managers are well aware of that, so their generosity is a sound business decision – especially in the winter.

We sit at the round table in the middle of the dining room with two officers: the ship's doctor, a personable young American, and the purser, a typically phlegmatic Dutchman who has such a voracious appetite that he always orders two portions of everything. We are joined by a good-natured little businessman from Philadelphia who has a weakness for champagne and whose mannerisms and mentality remind me of our businessmen back home, and by a spinster with a natural, amiable laugh, who dresses as expected of a woman of her age and class and is on her way home after visiting relatives in Holland. Since she lives on the Pacific coast, in the state of Washington, she still has to cross the entire continent after we land.

Many of the trips people take make no sense at all. My wife is beside herself over twin babies from Rotterdam whom we often see on deck in their carriages. Their mother is taking them to South Carolina to visit their grandmother, who insists on seeing her grandchildren – well and good, but it is so egotistical. South Carolina is farther south than Sicily – in June it's hotter than blazes, and if the babies get diarrhoea and start throwing up, what is their wilful grandmother going to say then? It is none of our business, of course, but when you are trapped in a confined space and you see things like that going on around you, you cannot help thinking about them.

The babies' nurse is Jewish and reads modern literature. Their mother takes her meals with her older siblings in a corner of the dining room not far from us, where the guests, like everybody else aboard ship, have become a familiar sight – it seems as if we have known them for ever. They are few in number and always the same. No one ever gets on or off the boat – I am just kidding of course – still, you catch yourself hoping to see a new face. There is a table with a group of young Dutchmen who are apparently on a pleasure cruise and often burst out laughing, and a fifth table where the captain dines with an older, distinguished-looking American couple. At teatime the couple sits ramrod straight, and after dinner they sit next to each other in the music room and read. That would account for everyone, if it were not for the boat's *enfant terrible*, a scrawny Yankee with protruding lips, the stereotypical Anglo-Saxon "fish lips" – beneath which British "bobbies" fasten their helmet's chin strap rather than under their chin – a man roughly in his mid-thirties who had asked for a table by himself, takes a book with him to read while eating and does not mix with the other passengers, but can be seen in tourist class playing shuffleboard with Jewish refugees. The other passengers consider his behaviour offensive and do not like him. I often saw him in his deckchair or at his table writing things in a notebook. Everyone thinks there is something wrong with him. You do not isolate yourself like that and then amuse yourself in tourist class. He must be a writer and have a serious problem with the way society is structured, though you would never know it from the socially acceptable dinner jacket he wears. I am a little envious of the way he insisted on having a table to himself and of the Jewish refugees whom he considers worthy of associating with. My pride says I am as capable of understanding the ideas he jots down in his notebook as they are, though I admit that at the moment I am more interested in aesthetic and psychological matters than in social issues.

I spent the day savouring Cervantes's epic wit, the sallies he describes in the second part of his book, or at least the way he frames them as a continuation of Don Quixote's literary fame: the popularity that Quixote and Sancho enjoy thanks to "their" novel, the grand history that depicts their comic adventures – the first part. The knight errant and his squire would never have been invited to stay in the duke and duchess's palace and amuse them if the royal couple had not already made their acquaintance in the book and were not delighted at the prospect of getting to know them in "real" life. This is a unique literary device. I know of no other novel in world literature where the hero's fame is based on his reputation's reputation. The technique of recurring characters in *Don Quixote* differs from that in novel cycles such as Balzac's.* In Balzac the characters' reality is legitimized, bolstered and enhanced by having them appear again and again to the reader, but the level they are depicted on never changes, the nature of the illusion remains the same. In Cervantes there is more involved: romantic illusion, ironic tricks. In the second part, Don Quixote and his squire leave the sphere of reality where they belonged and lived their lives – the novel – and, as representatives of an enhanced level of reality, cheered by the readers of their story, move in person into a world that like their own is linked to a former world, a world that exists in literature, on the printed page, and depicts a higher stage of reality, even though it too is a fictional world, an illusory evocation of a fictive past, allowing Sancho Panza to take the liberty of responding in jest when the duchess asks if Don Quixote is the same as the hero in *Don Quixote*, and instead says of himself, "And the squire of his who is, or ought to be, in that history, the one named Sancho Panza, is me unless I was changed for another in the cradle – I mean the printing press." Cervantes even brings in a figure that appears in the detested fake sequel and shows how it convinces itself in "real" time that the Don Quixote with whom it is paired in the story cannot possibly be the real one. These devices, like those used by E.T.A. Hoffmann,* had a profound influence on writers of the Romantic movement. Though they were not the greatest artists, they were the most productive thinkers on the uncanny, distorting mirrors and other artifices used to create illusion in art, and it is because they were artists in and beyond art that they came so dangerously close to the ironic dissolution of form. It is well to remember that the danger of this happening is inherent in every attempt to use humour as a device to persuade readers that what is depicted is real. It is a short step from the playfulness of certain literary devices to tricks of language and situation, to outright buffoonery that is devoid of form or a belief in form. So I am giving readers the unexpected opportunity to see, with their own eyes, Joseph, the son of Jacob, sitting near a well in the moonlight, the upper part of his body bare, and to compare him, attractive even if still an adolescent, with the idealized image that the centuries have woven around this famous figure.* I only hope that in having good-humouredly seized this occasion to portray the relationship between appearance and reality, I have kept within the bounds of what is considered acceptable art.

22nd May

We just keep on going, day after day, the engine never missing a stroke, as the ship navigates this expanse of ocean at the same steady pace. I enjoy taking my morning dip in the warm, sticky, slightly foul-smelling seawater pool, the pores of my skin absorbing the salt, and while relaxing in the brine I cannot help thinking that while we were asleep the ship covered a goodly stretch of infinity overnight. Meanwhile, the weather is starting to clear. Blue sky is peeking out from behind the clouds, painting the water with shafts of southern light, though the clouds soon devour the warmer light again.

In the early evening we like to stand on the boat deck with the wind in our faces, keeping watch as our ship sails west across the ocean. We always head towards the setting sun, and our course changes only slightly – yesterday we steamed directly into the sunset, and today we are deviating a little to the south. The movement of a ship through the ocean is a thing of beauty and a source of pride, more dignified and elegant than an express train rounding a curve, because it calls for the navigator to steer its course. The totality of the void in front of us is nothing short of breathtaking – even along "routes" used by ships belonging to the earth's seafaring nations. We are on our fourth day, but so far we have not seen the smoke of a single steamer. There is a simple explanation: too much open space. There is something cosmic about the length and breadth of the sea – the huge number of ships that ply the ocean disappear in it like stars in the sky, and it is only by chance that one meets another.

There is a reminder on the bulletin board to set our watches back each day, from half an hour to forty minutes – yesterday it was thirty-nine. Officially, the change takes place at midnight, but we perform this important ritual soon after dinner, to make sure that the night is not too long, the evening extended, and that we do not repeat the time we have already lived through when we read and listened to music. After some reflection, we decided to set the minute hands back again, for the third time in a day. Ten times thirty-nine minutes is six and a half hours that we are losing – no, gaining – on this voyage. Are we going back in time while moving forward in space? Absolutely – because our journey is westward, to where the sun sets, in a direction opposite to the earth's rotation. The word "cosmic", which I used earlier, is especially appropriate to our situation, because it shows how space and time have an impact on our consciousness in spite of the material comforts that insulate us from the elements, separating us from the raw power of nature. We are slipping into days that are unfamiliar to us, into regions of the earth's surface that, as they rotate around the sun, are exposed to its light at different times from those in otherwise inhabited parts of the globe and are still in darkness and asleep when the sun is shining back home. This is common knowledge, of course, but we give it a new twist. If we were to keep travelling west, so that we returned home from the farthest point in the east, we would gain the most time possible, as much as an entire day, totally confusing the calendar, but then lose it again in the end – win some, lose some. However, we are stuck now. If we do not take the long way home, we will just turn around and go straight back to our continent. But not to worry. Gaining time is not the same as gaining life – and if, after having arrived over there, we tried to outwit the cosmos, setting our watches neither forward nor backward and holding on jealously to our six hours, as Fafnir guarded his hoard,* our lifespans, organically embedded into the structure of the universe, would not be extended by a second.

What juvenile thoughts! Yet is there not also something puerile about the cosmological view of the universe when compared with its opposite, the psychological? I cannot help thinking of Albert Einstein's bright round eyes, like a child's. Deriving knowledge from the study of human beings, delving into their lives, reflects a more mature sensibility than speculations about the Milky Way – which I say with the utmost respect. "People," Goethe writes, "are free to study whatever excites them, whatever gives them pleasure, whatever they consider worthwhile, but the true study of humankind is man."*

As for *Don Quixote*, it is a curious work – naive, phenomenally spontaneous and unabashedly contradictory. I can only shake my head at the number of extraneous interpolated stories in the book. Sentimental and written in the Romantic mode that the author sets out to mock, these stories within stories offer readers an opportunity to feast themselves on the kinds of tales they are supposed to wean themselves from – what an enjoyable therapy! It is common knowledge that, after completing *Don Quixote*, Cervantes once again wrote perfectly crafted chivalric romances. Though not comfortable with the pastoral romance, he nevertheless continued writing them, if only to show that he could appeal to the literary tastes of the time and even become a master of the genre. On the other hand, I believe he is perfectly comfortable in having his hero deliver a humanistic discourse, making the novelistic figure exceed the limits of its intellectual capabilities and, in an "unartistic", mischievous way, putting his views into the mouth of his protagonist. Just the same, the views Quixote expresses are fascinating: for example, his reflections on education and his discourse on the nature and art of poetry to which he treats his travelling companion, the Knight of the Green Coat. Quixote's speeches are often filled with an abundance of pure reason, justice, human kindness and nobility of form. The Gentleman of the Green Coat "was so amazed at Don Quixote's words that he began to change his mind about his having to be a simpleton". Rightly so. In the same way, the author wants his readers to change their minds too. Although Quixote is no doubt unhinged, he is far from being a simpleton – something that even the author himself was not sure of in the beginning. Cervantes's respect for the creature of his own invention steadily increases as the story unfolds, a development that may be the most fascinating thing about the novel – a novel in itself – and that coincides with the growing respect he has for the work itself, which he originally intended as a crude satire, a jest, without any idea of the stature that his hero was destined to achieve as a symbol transcending a particular society and age. This shift of perspective causes and allows the author to identify himself with and support his hero, to assimilate his accomplishments with his own, to make him a spokesperson for his own convictions and opinions and to extend the intellectual and cultural reach of the chivalric charm that, despite his character's doleful appearance, is nevertheless manifest in Don Quixote's madness. It is his master's single-mindedness and use of language that are often the sources of Sancho's boundless admiration for him – as they also are for others.

23rd May

Less pitching and rolling. The weather is warmer, due to the Gulf Stream.

I begin my day by playing a fifteen-minute game of medicine ball with a steward from Hamburg who says he is a reader of mine. Ready for breakfast, I start off with half a grapefruit – a large variety of orange that is always available on board and is invariably of outstanding quality. To make it easier to eat, the cooks use a special implement to loosen the pulp from the peel. But I cannot get used to the chilled tomato cocktail that the Americans gulp down before every meal.

Since you have to get exercise, and walking non-stop around the promenade deck can be mind-numbing, we have taken up deck games and spent many hours in the morning and afternoon playing them. We play shuffleboard – a healthy and invigorating exercise – with a friendly young Dutchman. Rectangular courts are painted everywhere onto the promenade deck. You use a long stick with a curved tip to push a wooden disk inside a numbered section, making sure not to touch any lines or land it inside a menacing penalty area marked "10 off", while trying to slide a disk that missed its target into a scoring area – and, if possible, knock an opponent's disk out of a scoring zone. Easier said than done, and made even more difficult because of the unevenness of the court's surface – and, especially, the instability of the playing field, rising and falling with the motion of the ship, often making the game a matter of dumb luck. Taking your best shot does not help much: it is often a "shot in the dark", controlled by unpredictable forces, though your vexation at the loss of control gives you a certain emotional strength to try even harder, after which you feel you have earned your keep and deserve a hearty meal.

Deck golf, our other favourite game, is trickier than shuffleboard. It is played on a miniature golf course covered by artificial turf or other artificial surfaces. The player uses a putter to hit a ball from one of six starting points through a small hoop to a hole at the other end of the course in as few strokes as possible. In principle, it is possible to sink the ball with one stroke, at least from one of the centre positions, where the hoop and the hole are lined up together. But who manages to do that? Three strokes are considered honourable, two strokes brilliant. The worst foul-ups and ricochets usually happen near the hoop. After writing a six or seven on the scoreboard, you slink away as fast as you can.

At teatime and after dinner we usually sit in the Blue Salon, called "the Social Hall" here, and listen to the orchestra. Sometimes, especially in the afternoon, we are the only audience. On those occasions, the musicians play just for us, though we would be just as happy if they did not. But they need at least one guest in the hall to play. Sometimes, when we peer through the windows from the outside, we see them in the empty hall hanging around their music stands with blank looks on their faces, like unemployed workers who have given up hope looking for a job. But when a guest enters the hall, they immediately reach for their instruments and start to play.

The orchestra consists of a piano, two violins, a viola and a cello. The concertmaster leads the orchestra. The programme consists largely of light music – naturally. The high points are a pot-pourri from *Carmen* and a *Traviata* fantasy. Mostly, they play sugar-coated teatime pieces, poor imitations of the Puccini masterpieces that ordinary cultured people around the world enjoy listening to and are served up to them, especially during a crisis, so that, for a price, they can immerse themselves in music they are familiar with and feel secure. Everything on a voyage like this is designed to make you forget and stop thinking. But, being rebellious by nature, I sometimes gaze out the window in the Social Hall while the orchestra plays its overworked selections – part of the plan to divert us – and later I peer out the window on the promenade deck at the grey-green, whitecap-covered wilderness, and the horizon, as it rises slowly, pauses for a few seconds and sinks again.

We applaud the musicians, who are pleasantly surprised each time we do so and send the concertmaster to us to convey their thanks. Regardless of whether we thank them, they seem pleased with their performance, exchanging glances over this or that passage, discreetly talking shop, and having a good chuckle besides. When I look at them, I cannot help thinking you should be careful not to take these men too lightly. Although they sit there, performing this musical treacle – it is their job, after all – we know that if need be and worse comes to worst, they can just as well play 'Nearer, My God, to Thee'.* So you have to see them from that perspective too.

Now and then I dip into my little orange-coloured volume and am shocked to learn how cruel Cervantes can be. Even though, as I wrote yesterday, he identifies with and supports his hero and respects him, he never tires of finding ways to humiliate him and ridicule his generosity and magnanimity – as in the comical but lamentable incident of the curds that "that traitorous, shameless, discourteous" Sancho had placed in his master's helmet and that at the most embarrassing moment possible start to melt, so that the whey runs down Quixote's face and beard and makes him think his head is softening and that his brains are melting, or he's perspiring profusely, though he denies it has anything to do with being afraid. There is something sardonic and humorous in Cervantes's inventiveness in (to cite another example) the loathsome episode in which Quixote was "put in a wooden cage", locked inside and hauled home in a cart – the ultimate indignity. Quixote is continually assaulted and beaten up, almost as much as Lucius in *The Golden Ass*.* Even so, his creator loves and reveres him. Do not these beatings and assaults – all this cruelty – look like self-flagellation, self-mockery and self-incrimination? It seems to me as if someone is exposing to ridicule his own frequently flouted belief in the idea, in the human being, and his or her betterment, and that this painful coming to terms with common reality is the actual definition of humour.

As for translation, Cervantes puts an unparalleled critique in the mouth of his protagonist. Translating from one language into another, he says, is like looking at Flemish tapestries on the wrong wide, "for although the figures are visible, they are covered by threads that obscure them, and cannot be seen with the smoothness and colour of the right side... but I do not wish to infer from this that the practice of translating is not deserving of praise." What an amazing metaphor! Cervantes makes just two exceptions: the Spanish translators Figueroa* and Jáuregui.* In their case, as he puts it, you can happily not bring into question which is the translation and which the original. What extraordinary individuals they must have been! If I may, I would like, in Cervantes's name, to make another exception: Ludwig Tieck, who has added another *right* side to the tapestry we call *Don Quixote*, a German side.

24th May

Yesterday *The Golden Ass* came to mind and made its way into my pen, because I discovered certain affinities between *Don Quixote* and that ancient-Roman novel, though I must confess that I do not know if others have also been struck by them. The passages and episodes in Cervantes's novel I am referring to stand out because of their quirkiness and their bizarre motifs, which point to origins rooted in the distant past. It is also significant that they appear in the second, intellectually richer and profounder part of the book.

First: there is the account of the wedding of Camacho, "along with other agreeable events", in the second part, Chapter XXI. Agreeable? As the festivities at Camacho's wedding are in progress, things go terribly wrong – though the word "agreeable" in the chapter heading foreshadows that they are part of a ruse, a silly trick, a tragic hoax to fool the reader and the revellers, who in the end burst into bewildered laughter. The rustic wedding feast in honour of the fair Quiteria and the rich Camacho is described in a wealth of detail, as the happy Camacho celebrates his triumph over his rival Basilio, a valiant young man, who had been rejected by Quiteria – but only because she had been ordered by her father to do so, even though she has loved Basilio all her life, proving before God and man that she and Basilio rightly belong together. The festivities are about to end, and the wedding to begin, when the hapless Basilio appears "dressed in a black cassock decorated with fiery red strips", and in a hoarse, trembling voice says that because he alone is the obstacle standing in the couple's way he wishes to remove himself from the scene. "May the rich Camacho live with the thankless Quiteria for many long and happy years," he calls out, "and death, death to poor Basilio, whose poverty cut the wings of his contentment and sent him to the grave!" He pulls out a sword from the staff he had thrust into the ground, which served as a sheath, and, after placing the hilt in the ground, throws himself on the tip, so that half the blade emerges from his back and he lies on the ground bathed in his own blood.

It is hard to imagine a more horrific interruption of such a joyous and festive occasion. Everyone rushes over to help Basilio. Don Quixote himself leaves Rocinante to come to his aid, and the priest also comes over, though he asks that the sword not be removed until he hears Basilio's confession. But Basilio begins to revive and in a faint voice begs Quiteria to give him her hand in marriage in his final dying moment, because only then can he atone for his sin. What is he thinking? Does he really believe that Camacho is going to give up Quiteria because he is dying? The priest admonishes him to think of his soul and make his confession, but Basilio, his eyes turned up and evidently in his last throes, says he will not confess until Quiteria gives him her hand – what is at stake is a Christian soul that can be saved only when Camacho, a decent man, gives his permission. As soon as he receives the priest's blessing, Basilio jumps to his feet, pulls out the sword that had been sheathed in his body, and to those who begin to shout "A miracle, a miracle!" he replies "Not 'a miracle, a miracle' but ingenuity, ingenuity!" In short, the sword had passed not through Basilio's ribs, but through a hollow metal tube filled with blood – and the whole thing was a subterfuge concocted by the lovers, which, thanks to Camacho's good nature and Don Quixote's reasoning, ended with Basilio wedding Quiteria and Camacho insisting that the festivities should continue.

Is this fair? The suicide scene is treated with the greatest possible seriousness, as a genuine tragedy: it shocks and moves the onlookers, not to mention the reader – yet the whole affair ends in an atmosphere of cheer and good humour when the suicide is revealed as a piece of theatre. You cannot help being a little annoyed and wondering whether these kinds of tricks are appropriate for a work of art – or for art as we understand it. But I learn, from reading Rohde* and the excellent study on ancient Greek and ancient Near Eastern novels by the mythologist and historian of religion Karl Kerényi* in Budapest, that the novelists of late antiquity loved these kinds of stories. In his *Adventures of Leucippe and Clitophon*, Achilles Tatius* of Alexandria tells in barbaric detail the way the heroine, Leucippe, was sacrificed with almost sadistic cruelty by Egyptian Nile bandits. Witnessing the sacrifice from a trench separating him from his lover, Clitophon, anxious and distraught, goes over to Leucippe's grave to commit suicide. At that moment, Clitophon's friends, whom he thought were dead, hurry over and pull Leucippe, who is still alive, from her grave, and tell Clitophon that they had also been captured by the robbers and been forced to carry Leucippe to the place of sacrifice, where, to deceive the bandits, they gave her a sword that retreats into the sheath and completed their grisly task by providing her with a bladder of blood hidden under her robes. Am I wrong, or have not the blood-filled bladder and the whole blatantly contrived subterfuge set a precedent for *Don Quixote*?

Second: there is an incident reminiscent of Apuleius himself. I am referring to the unusual "Braying Adventure" in the second part, Chapter XXV. A donkey belonging to a village councilman has run off. And he and another councilman from the same village go into the woods, where they think the donkey is, but since they do not find it there, and because they are masters in the art of braying, they try to lure it into the open by imitating its loud, harsh cry. The first goes to one part of the woods and the second to another, one braying after the other, but when one of them hears the other braying, he comes running, thinking the donkey has returned, because he believes no one but a donkey could bray as well as he – and even though the councilmen continue to try to outdo each other in braying, they compliment and flatter each other on their special talent. The reason the donkey never comes is that it is lying in the woods, where the councilmen find it, torn apart by wolves. Disconsolate and hoarse, the two men return to their village. But the story of their braying spreads, and people in the village are taunted by people in the surrounding villages, who bray at them in mockery. Quarrels and armed clashes break out and spread from village to village, and just as the braying village sets off to do battle with another village, Don Quixote and Sancho Panza appear on the scene. In the mean time, the people in the braying village had made their mockery a badge of honour and a shield of pride, and with a braying donkey painted on a banner of white satin, and armed with lances, crossbows, pikes and halberds, they go to confront those who had insulted them and to do battle with them. Don Quixote approaches the offended villagers, stopping their advance. He makes a high-minded speech, calling on them in the name of reason to abandon their plan and avoid shedding blood for trifles. They seem willing to listen to him. But Sancho chimes in and ruins everything, telling them not only that it is foolish to lose your temper because you hear somebody bray, but also that when he was a boy he used to bray and did it so well that when he brayed all the donkeys in the village brayed, adding that if you know how to do it, it is like knowing how to swim: once you have learnt, you never forget. Then he holds his nose and begins to bray so enthusiastically that all the nearby valleys resonate with the sound – to his detriment. Because the villagers who cannot hear his explanation think he is mocking them, and they beat him senseless – and Don Quixote, who would normally have avenged his squire, flees to escape their crossbows and pikes and make himself scarce. The villagers put Sancho, who has only partly come to, "across his donkey", which will follow the trail of Quixote's horse. The men in the attacking squadron come back and spend the night waiting for the enemy that has never left its village, and they return to their own village joyful and proud, the learned author adding that "if they had known about the ancient custom of the Greeks, they would have raised a monument to their victory there and then."

A remarkable story! I believe I am not mistaken when I say that it resonates with a number of allusions to the past. The donkey plays a special role in ancient Greek and ancient Near Eastern theology. It is the visible manifestation of the Egyptian god Seth "The Red" (whom the Greeks called Typhon), the evil brother of Osiris, who continued to be an object of loathing well into the Middle Ages: rabbinic texts called Esau, Jacob's red-haired brother, a "wild donkey". The idea of beating was closely and sacramentally associated with the donkey, which is synonymous with phallic energy and the phallic organ. The phrase "beating the donkey" also has a cultic connotation. Entire herds of donkeys were ritually whipped and beaten as they were forced to go around city walls. And it was religious practice to throw a donkey over a cliff – the same kind of death Lucius, who had been transformed into a donkey in Apuleius's *Golden Ass*, barely escapes, the robbers having openly threatened him with *katakremnizesthai*.* Nevertheless, like Sancho Panza, he is beaten for braying and continues to be beaten as long as he is a donkey – fourteen occurrences in all. I might add that according to Plutarch the inhabitants of certain villages hated the donkey's cry so much that they banned trumpets because they sounded so much like braying.* Don't the villagers in *Don Quixote* sound a lot like those ancients, with their oh-so-sensitive ears?

It is strangely moving to see a Spanish Renaissance writer allude to our most ancient myths and present them to us cloaked in such innocent guises. Did he do so because of his knowledge of the novels of antiquity? Or did these themes come to him by way of Italy and Boccaccio? Let scholars decide.

The sky cleared as the day went on, and glowed a beautiful bright-blue hue. The sea is violet-coloured – isn't that how Homer described it? At noon we watched as the sun's rays illuminated massive banks of dense fog floating across the water, one after another, milky-white cushions for angels' feet to tread. A radiant, evanescent phantasmagoria.

The ship's doctor doesn't trust the weather. Yes, it's beautiful, he says, as long as the Gulf Stream keeps flowing, but you can't rely on it. Meanwhile, we enjoy the pleasant change: the warmer weather that tells us we are gliding into more southerly climes, the unsullied blue, the smoother sailing on a calm sea, the open boat deck, where we spend almost the whole day moving between sun and shade. You have to be careful, though: before you know it, you have a sunburn. Cool sea breezes can prevent you from feeling the heat, so the sun can do its damage without your knowing it.

Yesterday evening we watched a film in the Social Hall – the company makes sure we don't have to dispense with that gift of civilization either, while we are at sea, though it still seems strange to see a movie in the present circumstances. At one end of the hall a white screen was set up, and at the other that miraculous apparatus for projecting images and sound that evolved from the magic lantern of our childhood. You sit in the elegant Social Hall, which swayed slightly, dressed in your dinner jacket, ensconced in a lounge chair, at a little gilded table, drinking your tea, smoking your cigarettes, and, as in any Capitol or Eldorado Cinema on dry land, gazing at the moving and talking shadows in front of you – a very pleasant life. The lives the actors depicted on the screen are no less pleasant than our own, and equally elegant and comfortable. Since money is obviously no object, they can do whatever they wish, softening the blows, for themselves and for the audience, that are a natural part of life. Isn't that how things are meant to be? Movies are saturated with displays of wealth – spacious and elegant abodes, crystal serving dishes, tables piled high with fruit – to make ordinary people dream and to hold up a mirror to the possessing classes. The film we watched, originally American, told the story of an elderly executive with a dilettante's weakness for music, art, beauty and romantic passion who leaves his wife to pursue his dreams in Paris. However, his attempts to charm the woman of his dreams founder: she belongs to another man, a young musician whom he had supported and helped to become a success. The final shot shows him on the phone, calling his forgiving wife to tell her that he is coming home – a melancholy but not depressing ending, since we know that a spacious home and those crystal serving dishes are awaiting the return of a disillusioned but presumably wiser man.*

The sad thing was that there were so few of us to watch this pleasant, socially acceptable cinematic fantasy – just ten or twelve instead of hundreds in this luxury ocean liner's blue-and-gold Social Hall, the many unfilled voids reflecting an economic order that is coming apart at the seams. Not even all the members of our little group of stout-hearted regulars showed up. I missed the fish-lipped, note-taking American. Where was he? With the Jewish refugees in tourist class again? What an unsettling person. He travels first-class and takes his meals with us, wearing a dinner jacket, but makes it painfully obvious he has no desire to join in our intellectual conversations and retreats to an alien, hostile sphere. People should know where they belong. They should keep together.

"The Adventure of the Lions" is indisputably the watershed moment in Don Quixote's "exploits", and, in all seriousness, is likely the high point of the novel – a magnificent story told with a comic pathos that reveals the author's genuine love of his hero's foolish heroism. I immediately read it over twice and keep thinking of its strangely poignant, grandly humorous quality. The wagon with the flags on it and two lions from Africa inside "that the General of Oran is sending to the court as a present for His Majesty" is a delightful sight, and, if nothing else, a cultural artefact. Keeping the reader in suspense to learn more about Don Quixote's reckless magnanimity during this adventure – where, to the horror of his travelling companions, he refuses to allow himself to be "confused" by any reasonable objections to his mad intention – attests to the author's extraordinary ability to keep the novel's underlying psychological theme fresh and alive in all its variations and iterations. What is amazing about Don Quixote is that he is not so deranged that he is unaware of his own madness. "It is my rightful place," he says afterwards, "to attack those lions I attacked, although I know it was exceedingly reckless, because I know very well what valour means: it is a virtue that occupies a place between two wicked extremes, cowardice and temerity, but it is better for the valiant man to rise to the point of temerity than to lower to the point of cowardice – and just as it is easier for the prodigal to be generous than the miser, it is easier for the reckless man to become truly brave than for the coward." What moral intelligence! The Gentleman of the Green Coat's observation is no less fitting. Everything Don Quixote says, the Gentleman points out, is coherent and sensible, even though his actions are nonsensical, reckless and foolish. You almost get the impression that the author meant the conflict between Quixote's sane and insane self as a depiction of the natural and inevitable paradox inherent in a higher moral life.

The classical scene, captured in a hundred or more illustrations – where the lean-faced, dried-up hidalgo has leapt from his horse, fearing that his mare's courage might not measure up to his own, and takes up his battered shield and unsheathed sword, prepared to kill the ferocious beast in "combat", and stands before the wide-opened cage looking at it "attentively", observing the lion's movements and heroically and impatiently waiting to "tear it to pieces" – is truly extraordinary, and has come to life for me through Cervantes's vivid verbal portrayal, which goes on to describe the lion's gentle and embarrassing rejection of Don Quixote's challenge and show the knight errant acting as a hero more because he feels it is expected of him than because he wants to. The lion, who is not about to fall for Quixote's tricks and stratagems to provoke it, takes one look at him, turns around, exposes his "hindquarters" to the knight errant and with great placidity and calm goes back inside its cage and settles down. Quixote's heroics have been calmly and contemptuously ignored. The deplorable ridicule and scorn interwoven with the theme of rejection come crashing down on Don Quixote's head because of the majestic creature's disdainful indifference to his presence. Quixote is beside himself and orders the trembling keeper to hit the lion and provoke it into coming out, but the keeper refuses to do so and tells the knight errant that the greatness of his heart has been clearly demonstrated. No brave warrior to my understanding, the keeper says, is obliged to do more than challenge his opponent and wait for him in the field, and if his adversary does not appear, the dishonour lies with him. Don Quixote accepts the keeper's explanation and attaches to the end of his lance as a sign of victory the cloth he had used to wipe away the curds on his face. Seeing all this from afar, Sancho, who had left his master before his encounter with the lions, says, "Strike me dead if my master hasn't defeated the savage beasts, for he's calling us." A masterpiece of comic writing!

In no other place is the author's readiness to humiliate and, at the same time, exalt his hero more obvious than here. The twin concepts of humiliation and exaltation also reflect an important Christian experience and sensibility, and when merged with psychology and assimilated into the comic mode, they show how much *Don Quixote* is a product of Christian culture, Christian psychology and Christian humanity, and what Christianity means for the world of the mind, for poetry and humane values, and for valiantly spreading and upholding them. I cannot help thinking of my Jacob, humiliated and shamed, whimpering in the dust before the boy Eliphaz,* and how in a dream he arises, exalted, from the depths of his ultimately unsullied soul. Say what you will: Christianity, the flower that blossomed from Judaism, remains one of the two pillars on which Western civilization rests, the other being the ancient Mediterranean world. If any group or organization in the Western community of nations were to deny that one of these pillars is a source of our civilization and culture, not to mention both of them, it would mean that it had severed its ties with that community – which, thank God, is inconceivable and impossible – and would diminish any stature it could possibly have as a humane entity, leading to things that I cannot even begin to imagine. The vociferous attack on Christianity by Nietzsche, an admirer of Pascal, was an unnatural eccentricity, and is something I have always found disconcerting, like much else in this pathetic hero. Goethe, more balanced and not hobbled by any mental issues,* did not allow his "preference for paganism" to prevent him from paying homage to Christianity as the civilizing force that it is, and to regard it as an ally. Unsettled times like ours, which focus on momentous events rather than things of enduring meaning and value (for example, liberalism and freedom) – throwing out the baby with the bathwater – call for open-minded and resolute people, for people who refuse to "go with the flow", to go back to the foundations of our civilization, to reflect on them, to stand up for them, and to reject whatever threatens to undermine them. The criticisms levelled against Christian morality in our time (not to mention dogma and mythology), the reforms that attempt to bring it into conformity with life as it is lived, no matter how far-reaching or revolutionary they appear, are superficial. They fail to acknowledge what at the deepest level has caused Christianity to endure, has made it what it is today and has held it together over the centuries – the cultural Christianity of the West and the hard-fought and unalienable rights and values it stands for.

26th May

I am sorry to say that the ship's newspaper is a joke. It is published every day except Sunday, to make sure that we ocean-going travellers do not miss our freshly printed news any more than our freshly baked bread. It is slipped under our cabin door, where we find it and pick it up when we come down before lunch, and we read it straight away: we have just barely turned our backs on Europe, and who knows what it has been up to? Most of the paper – the ads and the pictures – is printed in advance, so it is not always up to date on the latest news. But the ship is equipped with a wireless. So, although we are seemingly alone and forsaken in the middle of this vast ocean, we are able to stay in touch with the rest of the world, send messages across the airways to all points on the compass and receive messages from anywhere and everywhere: news items wafted to our ship are plugged into the spaces made available for news in our paper. So what did we read today? A municipal zoo in the Western world prescribed whisky to treat a sick tiger, and the pernicious beast acquired such a taste for it that, even though fully recovered, it now demands a dram every day. News items like this are published regularly in the ship's paper. They are entertaining, of course. Not without good reason did the purveyors of our news think that we would develop a fondness for a tiger with a penchant for alcohol. But is this not a misuse of technology? Here you have a miracle of technology, such as radio telegraphy, and it is used to transmit this kind of "news" over land and sea. Ah, humanity! Its intellectual and moral progress has not kept pace with its technological advances – far from it. It is this dichotomy that fuels humanity's lack of faith in the idea that its future will be brighter than its past. It is this gap between technological maturity and a lack of maturity in other areas that accounts for the curiosity and wariness we feel when we reach for the latest issue of the ship's newspaper – and before we know it we are reading about a tiger that likes to get high on whisky. We are happy, of course, that we do not have anything worse to read about. Our wireless station's lack of seriousness reminds me a little of our ship's musicians. If need be, though, the station can still tap out an SOS signal. And you almost wish it would have occasion to do so, if only to protect technology's reputation.

Yesterday evening the wind came up and the ship pitched and rolled in the night, but today the weather is glorious again and as warm as on a summer's day. We saw a huge fish leaping above the water's surface. There is a rumour going around that at some point we ran over a whale, but it seems to be false. Still, since people think accidents like that are a natural occurrence during a sea voyage, they keep repeating it. On the other hand, the bar steward showed us a flock of seagulls in flight, swaying above the waves a short distance from the ship, a sign that land was not far off.

The hour and even the day of our arrival are still uncertain. We hear that, as long as the sea is calm and the weather good, the ship will land the day after tomorrow, Monday, in the afternoon. On the other hand, word has it that when we first set sail a dense fog had set in and delayed us, so it could be Tuesday by the time our ship pushes its way up the Hudson River. This uncertainty is one more example of what – to our benefit, I was about to say – distinguishes a sea voyage from travel by train. Despite all its conveniences and amenities, voyage at sea has preserved something primitive, primal, something left more to the elements, to chance, the approximate, which we feel instinctively drawn to and makes our trip so special. But why exactly? Is it that, even though I enjoy the comforts of civilized life, I also feel an aversion to mechanical civilization – a desire to reject it, repudiate it as a mortal threat to our souls and life itself, and instead to affirm and try to find a form of existence that is closer to the primitive, the primal, the elemental, the uncertain, the imprecise, the improvised, as in wartime, and the risky? But am I not at the same time becoming a voice for the increasingly universal appeal of the "irrational", for a cult that my critical sense has always regarded as a threat to humanity, especially because it is so susceptible to abuse, and which my European love of reason and order has always opposed – even more so, perhaps, because I feel like making up for the irrational drives within myself, the same kind I have worked so hard to combat in others? And, being a storyteller, I naturally turned to myth – and given my boundless contempt for Nordic–Germanic soulfulness and would-be barbarians, I humanize the mythical world and attempt to combine myth and humanity in a way I consider more hopeful for the future of mankind than the currently popular, one-sided efforts of those who deprecate the intellect and seek to ingratiate themselves with the powers that be by attacking reason and civilization. To set the groundwork for the future, it is not enough to be "in step with the time", along the lines of the movement *du jour*,* which is home to all those dimwits bursting with pride as they heap contempt on reactionary liberals, who are liberals of a very different sort.* You have to internalize the time in which you live, in all its complexity and with all its contradictions, because the future is born out of a multitude of possibilities, not just one.

Especially gripping and poignant are the scenes in *Quixote* that feature Ricote, a Morisco* and former shopkeeper in Sancho's village who had been forced to leave Spain when the king decreed the expulsion of the Moriscos.* Homesick for the land of his birth, Ricote sneaks back into his village, posing as a pilgrim, in hopes of recovering a secretly buried treasure. The chapter is a skilful blend of professions of loyalty to country, the author's affirmation of his Catholic orthodoxy, fulsome pledges of allegiance to the great King Philip III – and a deep sense of compassion for the dreadful fate of the Morisco community, which, without any regard for the suffering of the individual, had been so profoundly affected by the king's edict, sacrificed – presumably – for "reasons of state" and pushed into abject poverty. Cervantes's stance was a trade-off. By first expressing his loyalty to the powers that be, he gained permission to show empathy – and I believe it has always been felt that for him politics was a means to an end, to what really mattered to him: the right to express his true feelings. To help gain that permission, he even has the hapless Morisco voice approval of His Majesty's order, saying that it was "just and reasonable". Many of the Moriscos, the author has him say, refused to believe that the king was serious, and considered his proclamations a mere threat. But he, Ricote, knew immediately that these were real laws that would be mercilessly put into effect, and that he understood as much because he knew the "hateful and foolish intentions" of his fellow Moriscos were so heinous that it was divine inspiration that had moved His Majesty to put into effect "so noble a resolution". Those hateful and foolish intentions are never mentioned by name, and remain shamefully shrouded in darkness. So they stood unchallenged – even though, as Ricote says, not all Moriscos were guilty: some were firm and true Christians, but, sadly, he says, not many, so that the king was right to believe that it is not a good idea to nurture a snake in your bosom or shelter enemies in your house. The objectivity and moderation the author ascribes to the views of a figure so deeply affected by the expulsion are admirable. But, taken together, they drift imperceptibly into a different direction. It was just and reasonable, the Moor claims, to be chastised with the punishment of exile – lenient and mild, some say, although the most terrible we could have received. "No matter where we are, we weep for Spain – for, after all, we were born here, and it is our native country: nowhere do we find the haven our misfortune longs for, and in Barbary and all the places in Africa where we hoped to be received, welcomed and taken in, that is where they most offend and mistreat us." This Spanish "Moor" goes on to lament his fate bitterly, and it is impossible not to be moved by his laments. You do not know your good fortune, he says, until you lose it. The greatest desire in almost all of us is to return to Spain, and the desire is so great that we would abandon our wives and children and return even at the risk of our lives. That is how great our love for Spain is, and I now know from my own experience how sweet it is to love your country.

No one can fail to recognize that the intensity of Ricote's love of country and love of the land of his birth give the lie to the contrition expressed in phrases such as "a snake in your bosom", "enemies in your house" and the "nobility and justness" of the expulsion. The author's heart, as expressed in Ricote's speech in the novel's second part, speaks a more convincing language than the words that spill from his cautious, obsequious tongue: he has sympathy for the persecuted and the outcasts, who are good Spaniards like himself and were born in Spain, which will not be purer but poorer after they have been removed: Spain is their true, natural fatherland, and when uprooted from their native soil they will be outsiders everywhere else. Wherever they go, the words "at home" will be on their lips: "at home in Spain, it was thus and thus" – that is to say, better. Cervantes, impoverished freelance writer that he is, is forced to profess his loyalty, but no sooner does he deny himself the freedom to speak from his heart than he cleanses it more so than Spain, with all her edicts, cleanses herself ethnically. He condemns the cruelty and inhumanity of the laws he has just endorsed – not directly, but by stressing the exiles' love for their homeland. He even goes so far as to speak of "freedom of conscience". Ricote tells how he travelled to Italy and came to Germany, where he found he could live in greater freedom, because Germany, as he puts it, is a good, tolerant country and its inhabitants do not worry about "subtleties". Each man lives as he pleases, he goes on to say, and in most places there is freedom of conscience. So it was my turn to feel patriotic and proud, however old-fashioned those words sound. It has always been nice to hear a foreigner praise your country.*

27th May

The weather changes quickly near the sea, and even more quickly and erratically at sea, when a shift in atmospheric conditions merges with a slide into a different climate zone. By evening, after the sky had covered itself with clouds, yesterday's summer-like warmth gave in to an eerie sultriness – damper, thicker and heavier than I had ever experienced. My nerves got the better of me, so that I half expected a monstrous storm to come up or some other catastrophe to happen. My evening clothes weighed heavily on me. I sat drenched in sweat under my starched shirt, and a cup of tea caused a waterfall of perspiration to cascade from every pore. I do not remember how far into the night it lasted, but today it is over. This morning it was cool and rainy: fog rolled in, and the foghorn kept blasting for hours. But then it suddenly stopped. The wind sprang up, the fog lifted and the sky cleared, and even though the sun was shining, it remained – at least in comparison with yesterday evening's tropical weather – so cool that you had to wear a coat and wrap yourself in a blanket to lie in a deckchair.

There is a hint of excitement at the prospect of our arrival. It is Sunday. And word has it we will arrive in the night, between tomorrow and the day after, but until tomorrow we will be anchored at the mouth of the Hudson River before we dock on Tuesday around seven in the morning.

I feel I have to return to what I wrote yesterday to justify my claim that the commitment of *Don Quixote*'s author to Christianity and his allegiance to the Crown greatly enhance the value of his spiritual and intellectual freedom. In particular, I am concerned with the relativity of freedom, the fact that it needs to be countervailed by strong constraints and limitations – and not just those imposed from outside, but also those coming from within, so that it can become a true spiritual value and an expression of a more elevated way of life. It is hard to imagine the state of semi-feudal dependence in which artists in the past lived before the emancipation of their personal identity, a development that was ushered in during the bourgeois period, but that only rarely – and then only in the case of just a few great artists – benefited the artist as a category. Loosely modelled on handicraft guilds, associations of artists, including guilds of master artists and their students, only occasionally produced individual artists who, because of their good fortune and skill, were allowed to enter the presence of the sovereign and become outstanding intellectuals in their own right. Developments such as these were, on the whole, more beneficial to the well-being of artists than starting off by emancipating the individual, giving him his freedom and sovereignty and creating conditions in which humility and modesty are no longer the seedbeds of greatness. Traditionally, a prospective painter or sculptor who was intent on dedicating himself to adorning and beautifying the world and wanted to learn the artistic profession would apprentice himself to a successful master and begin his career by washing brushes and grinding pigments. He would become a valuable assistant to the master, who would eventually allow him to fill in or complete parts of a work, like a professor of surgery who says to his assistant at the end of an operation: "You finish!" If all went well, an apprentice would become a master artist – producing works of his own, as he had always wanted to do. He would be called *artista* – a word that linked two concepts, that of artist and artisan, and that even today is used in Italy for anyone skilled in a particular craft. The genius – the creative ego that boldly sets out on his own – is the exception, as he transitions from a traditional handicraft culture, decorative and utilitarian, into a world of kings and princes where, even though granted noble status and elevated to new heights, he is still a son of the Church and has to produce works of art that the Church commissioned. Nowadays, as I have indicated, we assume that the lone genius – the individual ego, the solitary spirit and intellect – is the model and the fount of culture, which is clearly an unhealthy state of affairs. The poet Hugo von Hofmannsthal,* who had a close personal connection to the eighteenth century because of his partial Italian heritage, once explained to me, in his brilliantly witty way, the profound changes that had taken place in those days in the way in which musicians viewed life. If you went to see a master musician, he would say: "Do sit down. Would you like a cup of coffee? Do you want me to play something for you?" That is how artists behaved back then. "Today they all look like sick eagles."* Precisely. Artists have become sick eagles, because art has become such a solemn affair and artists have – on average – been put on a pedestal, in a truly unfortunate way, and treated as melancholy figures, isolated and misunderstood – that is, they have become "sick eagles".

The poet and the writer represent a type of art that differs from that of the visual *artista* and the musician, so poetry and works of literature have a special place among the arts because they are not so much a craft – at least not in the common sense of the word – as they are a more spiritual endeavour, and their relationship to the spirit and the intellect is, on the whole, more direct. Poets and writers are not just artists – or, rather, they are artists of a different, more spiritual kind, since their medium is the word and the tools of their craft are spiritual and intellectual. So in their case, as in that of others, it would be desirable if their liberation and emancipation were to come at the end of a developmental process rather than at the beginning, if they were to evolve, like humanity in general, from subservience, suppression, bondage and dependency. Once again: freedom is only valued or revered when it has been won, when it is freedom from, the result of liberation. Cervantes's sympathy for the fate of the Moors, his implicit criticism of the cruelty inherent in "reasons of state", are all the more powerful and intellectually compelling because they are preceded by displays of subservience and so are not hypocritical, but rather signs of intellectual integrity! Human dignity and freedom, the emancipation of artists of the soul and mind, genuine spiritual boldness, are brought to light in a quixotic blend of cruel, demeaning ridicule and sublime tenderness, all of which – creative genius, sovereign individuality, the highest possible goals – rest on respect and reverence for the Office of the Holy Inquisition, pledges of loyalty to the monarch and acceptance of the "well-known generosity" of some of Spain's most powerful patrons, like the Count of Lemos and Bernardo de Sandoval y Rojas, the Archbishop of Toledo. At the same time, and similar to the way in which he spontaneously and unexpectedly moved away from the limitations imposed by his professions of loyalty to Crown and Church, Cervantes's work, originally conceived to do no more than satirize for simple comic effect, moved beyond its modest beginning to become a classic that is read with delight by generations of readers and has become an emblem of the human condition. I think it is the rule rather than the exception that the great books are the result of modestly declared intentions. Ambition should not precede the writing of a work – rather, it should grow as the work grows, as it takes on a life of its own, greater than the blithely astonished artist ever imagined: ambition is part of the work and unconnected to the artist's ego. Nothing is more pernicious than abstract and a-priori ambition, ambition per se, independent of the work, the sallow ambition of the ego. An artist whose ego is possessed by that kind of ambition sits there like a "sick eagle".

28th May

Last day on board. Yesterday we saw a ship, the first since we left Europe – it was a big event. It was a Danish vessel, about the same size as ours, flying the Dannebrog from its stern. I enjoyed watching our ship dip its ensign in salute, a chivalrous sign of respect that vessels everywhere pay one another in passing. From the bridge a whistle sounded, and a sailor hurried to lower our Dutch colours to half mast while the Dannebrog was drawn down on the other vessel. After we passed, the whistles blew again, and the flags were raised back up, the rules of nautical etiquette having been duly observed. What a charming custom! The sailors who work on ships such as these are united in fellowship by their unique profession and inspired by a spirit of adventure, in spite of mechanization, and by the respect they pay to one another when they meet in the vast, turbulent environment they share and are committed to, setting an example for the nations of the world – whose ships are ambassadors and extensions of their national territory – to do as they do and behave civilly towards one another, as long as they are not at war. Denmark and the Netherlands, of course, are not likely to wage war against each other. They are small, rational countries, and have been relieved of the burden of their heroic pasts, whereas the great powers are always thinking about war, so that when they dip their flags they might, ironically, be using an ancient act of courtesy to conceal their real intentions.

The sky is bright and sunny, the sea rippled gently. The ship moves quietly, swaying slightly from side to side, probably because of the course we are steering. Compared with the tropical weather we had in the evening the day before yesterday, the change in temperature is astounding. The night was cold, the morning more than brisk, so that even now when you lie in a deckchair, in the sun, you need a blanket and an overcoat.

I am tempted to call the ending of *Don Quixote* a little weak. Quixote's death seems to have been written mainly to protect the figure from any future unauthorized use and prohibit any potential unauthorized continuation of the story, but in doing so it comes across as contrived, as an overt literary device, and is not convincing. There is a difference between a beloved character dying as a natural consequence of the author's narrative and the author's killing him off, ordering and trumpeting its death, so that no one else can bring it back to life. Quixote's death is an elaborately staged event born of jealousy – jealousy that reflects the author's pride in identifying himself with and defending the remarkable and enduring creation of his unusually inventive imagination, an emotion that is not any less sincere because it is expressed in comic devices used to safeguard that creation from others' attempts to revive it. The priest asks a scribe to draw up a document to the effect that Alonso Quixano the Good, commonly called Don Quixote of La Mancha, has passed from this life and has died a natural death, and is requesting the document "in order to remove the possibility that any author other than Cide Hamete Benengeli will falsely resurrect him and write endless histories of his deeds". But Cide Hamete Benengeli vanishes, only to turn up as the comic device he always was and still is. He hangs his pen on a copper wire and warns presumptuous and unscrupulous historians before they take it down and profane it:

> Careful, careful, worthless idlers!
> Let no one lay a hand on me;
> for this enterprise, O king,
> is reserved only for me.

Who is speaking? Who is saying "for me"? The pen? No, it is someone else. "For me alone was Don Quixote born, and I for him; he knew how to act, and I to write; the two of us alone are one, despite and regardless of the false Tordesillan writer who dared, or will dare, to write with a coarse and badly designed ostrich feather about the exploits of my valorous knight, for it is not a burden for his shoulder or a subject for his cold creativity." Magnificent! The author knows what a noble and heavy burden he had shouldered in creating this universally loved history, even though at the beginning he was not aware of it. How strange! At the very end, though, he is either still not aware of it or he has forgotten it.

He says: "For my only desire has been to have people reject and despise the false and nonsensical histories of the books of chivalry which are already stumbling over the history of my true Don Quixote, and will undoubtedly fall to the ground. *Vale*." This is a reversion to the book's original, modest intention of simply being a social satire, a parody that unexpectedly far outstripped anything the author had originally intended – and the death scene itself is a representation of that reversion, because it is preceded by a conversion. After sleeping more than six hours, the dying knight errant awakens to find that, blessed be Almighty God, his "judgement is restored" and has been cleared of the dark shadows imposed by the constant reading of detestable books of chivalry, and that he now understands their absurdities and deceptions and no longer wants to be Don Quixote of La Mancha, the Knight of the Sorrowful Face, the Knight of the Lions, but rather Alonso Quixano, a reasonable human being, a human being like any other. That should make us happy. But, surprisingly, it does not – rather, it makes us think more dispassionately and objectively, so that we are saddened in a way. We feel sorry for him, just as we were saddened to see the way the melancholy caused by his final and irremediable defeat extended to his deathbed and ultimately his death. Indeed, the doctor who attended him diagnosed the cause of his imminent death as melancholy and grief. What finally kills him is the deep depression that results from the realization that his mission as a knight errant to redress wrongs and restore justice has failed, and we – who still hear that weak and feeble voice that said, "Dulcinea of Toboso is the most beautiful woman in the world, and I am the most unfortunate knight on earth, and it is not right that my weakness should give the lie to this truth. Wield your lance, knight!" – we feel his dejection, even though we know that his mission had to end as it did, since it was a product of his madness and lunacy. Yet, as the story unfolds, his mad pursuit of justice becomes so endearing that we are tempted and prepared to let it stand as a sign of the human spirit, to feel as if it is the very embodiment of that spirit – for which we are deeply indebted to the author.

Don Quixote is one of the most difficult and challenging works of fiction, because it is unbalanced. If it had remained faithful to its original intention of parodying chivalric romances by simply depicting the ridiculous exploits and defeats of a madman, things would have been simple. But because it exceeded its original intention, it was deprived of a satisfying ending. It was unthinkable to have Don Quixote defeated and killed in one of his mad sallies – and it would have been in bad taste to make an extended joke out of his fortuitous madness. Having him live on after he had come to his senses would also have been out of the question: it would have been like having the character sink back into his former self, having him live on as an empty husk without a soul, apart from the fact that he had to die in order to protect an original work of literature. I also understand that it would not be Christian or edifying to allow him to die in pursuit of his chivalric delusion, to be saved from the lance of the Knight of the White Moon only to live on in deep despair over his final and irretrievable defeat. The only way to end this despair was to make him realize that he was mad and have him recover his sanity on his deathbed. On the other hand, it is also possible that he died of despair only after realizing that Dulcinea was not a beautiful princess, but rather a dirty little peasant girl, and that everything he believed in and suffered for, and all his actions, were pointless. What is certain is that it was imperative to save Don Quixote's soul for the sake of sanity before he died. But to have his salvation truly resonate with us, the author should not have made his madness as engaging as he did.

It is obvious that even geniuses can find themselves in a quandary and an author's plan go awry. Even so, Cervantes does not make much of Don Quixote's death. He has his passing celebrated like that of any other respectable citizen, in a dignified and Christian manner, after he had made his confession, tended his soul and asked a scribe to draw up his final will and testament. "Since human affairs, particularly the lives of men, are not eternal and are always in a state of decline from the beginnings until they reach their final end, and since the life of Don Quixote had no privilege from Heaven to stop its natural course, it reached its end and conclusion." Like the friends and family he leaves behind – his housekeeper, his niece and Sancho, his squire – the reader cannot help but see his passing in a comic way. They mourn him deeply, showing the reader once again what a good man he was, and the news of his imminent death is described grotesquely as "terrible pressure being put on already full eyes", forcing "tears from their eyes and a thousand deep sighs from their bosoms". Sincere grief is also depicted in a slightly burlesque tone: we are told that although the whole house was in an uproar during the three days of Don Quixote's death throes, human nature and practicality dictated that his niece ate, his housekeeper drank and Sancho Panza was happy, "for the fact of inheriting something wipes away or tempers in the heir the memory of the grief that is reasonably felt for the deceased". This "realistic", unsentimental observation was likely considered shocking at the time. However, it once again shows that a sense of humour is and has always been the boldest and bravest conqueror in the realm of human affairs.

Six o'clock in the afternoon. We've finished packing. With our trunks on the floor and no stands to put them on, it was a big job. The passengers can hardly wait for the ship to dock. We watch as it closes to the pier and the crew is busy securing ropes. From the expressions on their faces we can tell how eagerly our American fellow passengers are looking forward to returning to their own country, to coming home – sadly, we have the opposite feeling.

It is evening. To the right of our slowly moving vessel, the lights of the Long Island shoreline, with its celebrated beaches and summer residences, grew brighter in the night sky. Since we have to get up early tomorrow, we go to bed early. The readiness is all.

The weather is still fine, brisk and slightly misty. At half-past five in the morning we say goodbye to the narrow beds that had rocked like hammocks for so many nights. Our ship, which had dropped anchor the night before and allowed us for the first time to sleep without the rumble and vibration of its engines, has slowly started to move again. We had breakfast, gave the last touches to our luggage and handed out the final tips. Set for our arrival, we go on deck to watch the ship enter port. In the distance a familiar figure rises from the mist – the Statue of Liberty, with her crown – a figure in neoclassical style, a symbol of naive optimism that, sadly, has become an anomaly in today's world...

I feel a little woozy, either from getting up so early or because of something peculiar about that time of day. I also had a dream during the night – since the ship's engines had stopped, I was not used to the silence. I am trying to recall the dream. It revolved around what I had read during the voyage. I dreamt of Don Quixote, the knight errant himself, and I spoke with him. But since reality differs from what we think it to be, he looked different from the figure depicted in illustrations: he had a thick, bushy moustache, a high forehead and, beneath his equally bushy eyebrows, grey, half-blind eyes. He did not call himself Alonso Quixano the Good, but rather Zarathustra. Now that we met face to face, he was so gentle and gracious that I was moved beyond description by the words I had read about him yesterday: "Whether Don Quixote was simply Alonso Quixano the Good, or whether he was Don Quixote of La Mancha, he always had a gentle disposition and was kind in his treatment of others, and for this reason he was dearly loved not only by those in his household, but by everyone who knew him." Anguish, love, compassion and unbounded veneration filled my heart, and have become a reality for me, pulsating dreamily within me in this, the hour of our arrival.

But these thoughts and feelings are much too European and point in the wrong direction. In front of us, Manhattan's skyscrapers rise out of the early morning mist – a dramatic landscape, a vast metropolis of towering buildings.

Notes

p. 8, *New Amsterdam*: The Dutch settlers' name for New York, changed by the English in 1664.

p. 9, *the time the Russian writer Ivan Goncharov... high seas*: In the autumn of 1852, the Russian author Ivan Goncharov (1812–91), who would later become famous for his novel *Oblomov* (1859), was invited by Admiral Putyatin (1803–83) to join him as his secretary on an expedition to the Far East on board the frigate *Pallada*, calling at London and Cape Town before sailing on to Java, Singapore, Hong Kong, Japan, Shanghai, the Philippines and Korea. Goncharov kept detailed log and diary entries and wrote letters home to friends recounting his experiences – material which would later form the basis of a full-length account of his voyage, *The Frigate Pallada* (1858).

p. 18, *"It is beautiful of course... to be them"*: The quotation is from Schopenhauer's *The World as Will and Idea* (Chapter 46, 'On the Vanity and Suffering of Life').

p. 19, *a poem that Tonio Kröger addressed to the sea but could not finish*: The quotation is from Chapter 7 of Mann's 1903 novella *Tonio Kröger*.

p. 19, *Hans Castorp's splendid lounge chair in The Magic Mountain*: A reference to a passage in Chapter 3 of

Mann's 1924 novel *The Magic Mountain*, whose protagonist is the tubercular young man Hans Castorp.

p. 20, *Tieck's translation*: The German poet Ludwig Tieck (1773–1853) published a celebrated translation of *Don Quixote* between 1799 and 1801.

p. 21, *plagiarized sequel*: A spurious sequel of *Don Quixote*, written pseudonymously under the name Alonso Fernández de Avellaneda, was published in 1614. Cervantes went on to publish his own sequel in 1615, ten years after the publication of the first part.

p. 21, *the Battle of Lepanto*: A naval engagement – the largest in Western history since classical antiquity – that took place on 7th October 1571, when a fleet of the Holy League, a coalition of Catholic states, inflicted a major defeat on the fleet of the Ottoman Empire [TRANSLATOR'S NOTE].

p. 25, *even if that success is initiated by a crime*: Likely an allusion to the Night of the Long Knives (30th June to 2nd July 1934), when Hitler ordered a series of extrajudicial killings [TRANSLATOR'S NOTE].

p. 30, *Küsnacht near Zürich in Switzerland*: At the time of Hitler's rise to power in 1933, Mann was on a lecture tour in Switzerland. His children Erika and Klaus, who had remained in Munich, contacted their father with a warning not to return to Germany, and as a result he moved to Küsnacht on Lake Zurich, where he lived for five years until 1938.

p. 31, *baked Alaska*: "A dessert consisting of sponge cake and ice cream covered with meringue, cooked in a hot oven for a very short time so that the ice cream does not melt" (*OED*).

p. 34, *novel cycles such as Balzac's*: In Balzac's novel cycle *La Comédie humaine* ("The Human Comedy"), which includes over ninety finished works, several characters reappear in multiple stories.

p. 35, *E.T.A. Hoffmann*: The German Romantic writer E.T.A. Hoffmann (1776–1822), famous for his Gothic horror stories and fantastic tales.

p. 36, *Joseph... this famous figure*: A reference to a scene in the chapter "Fame and the Present" in Mann's novel *The Stories of Jacob* (1933), the first part of his tetralogy *Joseph and His Brothers* (1933–43).

p. 41, *as Fafnir guarded his hoard*: Fafnir is a character in Norse mythology. In the Völsunga saga (13th century), he appears as the son of Hreithmar, who had demanded a vast amount of gold from Odin as a compensation for the loss of one of his sons. Fafnir kills his father in order to secure the gold, but Odin puts a curse on it. Fafnir then changes into a dragon to guard his hoard, until he is slain by the hero Sigurd.

p. 41, *"People... is man"*: From Goethe's 1809 novel *Elective Affinities* (Part Two, Chapter VII). The last part of Goethe's quotation is in turn derived from Alexander Pope's famous dictum "The proper study of mankind is man" (*An Essay on Man* II, l. 2).

p. 50, *'Nearer, My God, to Thee'*: A nineteenth-century Christian hymn by Sarah Flower Adams (1805–48). Allegedly, it was the last song played by the band on the *Titanic* before its sinking.

p. 50, *The Golden Ass*: A novel by Apuleius (*c.*124–after 170), also known under the title *The Metamorphoses*.

p. 51, *Figueroa*: Cristóbal Suárez de Figueroa (1571–1644), translator of *Il pastor fido* (1590) by Giovanni Battista Guarini (1538–1612).

p. 51, *Jáuregui*: Juan de Jáuregui (1583–1641), translator of Tasso's *Aminta*.

p. 57, *Rohde*: The German classical scholar Erwin Rohde (1845–98), who wrote an important study of the ancient novel [TRANSLATOR'S NOTE].

p. 57, *Karl Kerényi*: The Hungarian classical scholar and philologist Károly Kerényi (1897–1973), who published his German works under the name Karl Kerényi. The "excellent study" referred to is *The Greek-Oriental Romances in the Light of the History of Religions* (1927), Kerényi's first published book, from which Mann draws the subsequent classical references.

p. 57, *Achilles Tatius*: An author who is believed to have flourished in the second century AD.

p. 60, *katakremnizesthai*: Κατακρημνίζω, an archaic form of capital punishment, in which the victim was thrown down a rock or precipice [TRANSLATOR'S NOTE].

p. 60, *according to Plutarch... so much like braying*: The story, reported in Kerényi's book, is narrated in Plutarch's *Moralia* ("On the Worship of Isis and Osiris", 30): "The people of Busiris and Lycopolis do not use trumpets at all, because these make a sound like an ass."

p. 62, *The film we watched... wiser man*: Mann probably saw the American film *A Parisian Romance* (1932), directed by Chester M. Franklin (1889–1954) and starring Lew Cody (1884–1934), Marion Shilling (1910–2004) and Gilbert Roland (1905–94). Based on an 1890 play by the French writer Octave Feuillet (1821–90), the film is about an elderly Parisian rake, a baron (not an elderly American businessman) who tries to win a young girl (Claudette) away from her fiancé (Victor), a struggling young artist, but ends up feeling morally obliged to break his engagement to her. As the film ends, he picks up the phone, just like in Mann's depiction – not to speak with his wife, but rather to re-engage with one of his former sweethearts. The discrepancies between Mann's description and the actual plot may have been caused by the author's tenuous knowledge of the English language at the time.

p. 65, *my Jacob... Eliphaz*: A reference to the chapter "Eliphaz" in *The Stories of Jacob* (see note to p. 36).

p. 66, *not hobbled by any mental issues*: Nietzsche famously suffered from mental illness and died in a lunatic asylum.

p. 74, *du jour*: "Of the day" (French).

p. 74, *who are liberals of a very different sort*: Reactionary liberals believe in a union of economic policies typical of liberalism (e.g. free enterprise) with traditionalist social values and in a democratic form of government [TRANSLATOR'S NOTE].

p. 74, *a Morisco*: Muslims were known by Spaniards as "Moors". Moriscos were former Muslims and their descendants, whom the Roman Catholic Church commanded to convert to Christianity [TRANSLATOR'S NOTE].

p. 74, *the expulsion of the Moriscos*: This was decreed by King Philip III of Spain (1578–1621) on 9th April 1609.

p. 77, *to hear a foreigner praise your country*: The expulsion of the Moriscos from Spain in 1609 was clearly mirrored, around the time of Mann's voyage (1934), by the fate of the Jews who were being driven out of Germany (the Nuremberg Race Laws of the following year would make Jews legally different from their non-Jewish neighbours). Mann, however, decided not to draw open parallels between the two events.

p. 83, *Hugo von Hofmannsthal*: The Austrian playwright and librettist Hugo von Hofmannsthal (1874–1929), whose father was half Austrian, half Italian.

p. 83, *they all look like sick eagles*: The term "sick eagle" was coined by Hofmannsthal to ridicule the creative ego of the late nineteenth century's cult of genius, of the artist who had no choice between being a genius or nothing [TRANSLATOR'S NOTE]. The expression is possibly a nod to a sonnet by Keats, the melancholy poet par excellence: "My spirit is too weak: mortality / Weighs heavily on me like unwilling sleep, / And each imagined pinnacle and steep / Of godlike hardship tells me I must die, / Like a sick eagle looking at the sky" ('On Seeing the Elgin Marbles', ll. 1–5).

Extra Material

on

Thomas Mann's

*A Voyage at Sea
with Don Quixote*

Thomas Mann's Life and Works

Paul Thomas Mann was born in the Hanseatic city of Lübeck on 6th June 1875, the second son of Thomas Johann Heinrich Mann and his wife Júlia da Silva Bruhns. His father Thomas Johann was a grain merchant and a senator of the city, while his mother came from a German-Brazilian family. His maternal grandfather had moved to Brazil, where he married and had five children. It seems he also had a child with his daughter's Afro-Brazilian nanny. It is not known if the wider family was aware of this. Júlia and her siblings moved to Germany when she was seven years old, and she later published memoirs of her upbringing.

The other children in the Mann family were: Heinrich (1871–1950), Julia (1877–1927), Carla (1881–1910) and Viktor (1890–1949). Heinrich Mann became an important writer: his most famous works are *Professor Unrat* (*Small-Town Tyrant*) which was adapted for film as *Der blaue Engel* (*The Blue Angel*), starring Marlene Dietrich, and *Der Untertan* (*Man of Straw*, also known as *The Loyal Subject*). Julia wrote short prose and journalistic pieces, while Viktor published his memoirs of the family. Carla became an actress and committed suicide at the age of twenty-nine. This episode may have been the inspiration for the character of Meta Mackedey in Thomas Mann's 1947 novel *Doctor Faustus*.

From 1882 to 1891 Thomas attended the Katharineum, a grammar school in Lübeck. He was not a successful pupil, and had to repeat various years. He never obtained his diploma (*Abitur*). During this time, he became friends with Otto Grautoff, with whom he shared many of his early secrets. When he was sixteen, Thomas fell in love with a fellow pupil, Armin Martens, but was ridiculed when he confessed his feelings. He later had a crush on another fellow pupil called Willri Timpe, from whom he wanted to borrow a pencil. His first love became the model for Hans Hansen in the novella *Tonio Kröger* (1903). The episode with the borrowed pencil returns in *The Magic Mountain* (1924), where Willri becomes Pribislav Hippe, the first erotic interest of the novel's protagonist Hans Castorp.

Together with his friend Otto Grautoff, Thomas read and discussed *Psychopathia Sexualis* (1886), an influential study of sexuality by Richard von Krafft-Ebing. In it, homosexuality is described as a pathology, and gay men are referred to as "stepchildren of Nature". The author explains that it is possible to be "cured", and he cites numerous cases. Otto Grautoff, who was also gay, later underwent a form of what we would now call "conversion therapy". He married and became an art historian and translator; he founded the *Deutsch-Französische Gesellschaft* ("German-French Society") after the First World War in order to foster relations between the two countries. In their last year at school, Thomas and Otto published a literary magazine called *Frühlingssturm* ("Spring Storm").

While Thomas was still at secondary school, his father's business was liquidated and the family house was sold. A year later, in 1891, his father died, and soon afterwards his mother moved to Munich with her younger children. Heinrich had already moved out and worked and studied in Berlin. Thomas would follow his mother to Munich in 1894. He worked at an insurance firm for a while, but his dream was to follow in his brother Heinrich's footsteps and become a writer. The same year he moved to Munich, his first story, 'Gefallen'("Fallen"), was published in a local magazine, *Die Gesellschaft*.

Between 1895 and 1898, he accompanied his brother Heinrich, with whom he would have a difficult relationship throughout his life, on various trips to Italy, staying in Palestrina, near Rome, for long periods of time. He also contributed to a nationalist and anti-Semitic magazine: *Das zwanzigste Jahrhundert* ("The Twentieth Century"), of which Heinrich was editor-in-chief for a short while. He would later distance himself from the publication and call it *"ein reaktionäres Wurschtblatt"* ("a reactionary rubbish magazine"). During his stay in Italy, he conceived the idea of writing a family chronicle, initially as a cooperation with his brother.

It took Thomas a few years and multiple rejections before he was able to follow up on his early success as a published writer. In 1896 he managed to get his second story printed in the recently founded magazine *Simplicissimus*. It was called 'Der Wille zum Glück' ("The Will to Happiness"). This story was followed by 'Der kleine Herr Friedemann' ("Little Herr Friedemann"), published in *Neue Deutsche Rundschau* in 1897. The same magazine also published his novella *Tonio Kröger* in 1903. His stories and novellas soon appeared in book form too. Samuel Fischer published two collections, each containing six stories or novellas: *Der kleine Herr Friedemann* (1898) and *Tristan* (1903).

Around this time Thomas was called up for military service. After only a few months in the army, however, he was declared unfit for service and discharged. Meanwhile, he had been working on his first great novel, *Buddenbrooks*. To write it, he used copious notes about his family's history his sister Julia had sent him. Despite some hesitation about its length, it was published by Samuel Fischer in 1901. A more affordable one-volume edition was published in 1903, which became a literary success.

In 1900 Thomas met the painter Paul Ehrenberg, with whom he secretly fell in love. They became friends and were often accompanied by Paul's brother Carl, who was a musician. One of his letters to the Ehrenberg brothers was signed "Tonio Kröger", his alter ego from the novella based on his first love. This novella was dedicated to Kurt Martens, a friend who had "overcome" his homosexuality and was married, just like Otto Grautoff. Thomas seemed to have decided that he wanted to follow his friends' example. In 1903 he met Katia Pringsheim, the daughter of a wealthy Jewish entrepreneur and professor of Mathematics. She was one of the first women allowed to study at the University of Munich (Physics and Mathematics), and had a twin brother who was gay. Thomas and Katia married in 1905. In 1908 they bought a property in Bad Tölz in the Bavarian Alps, where they had a summer house built.

A year after his marriage, in 1906, Thomas published 'Wälsungenblut' ("The Blood of the Walsungs"), a story in which a Wagner-loving, German-Jewish twin brother and sister called Siegmund and Sieglind have sex on a polar-bear rug shortly before Sieglind's wedding.

A few years later, in 1909, Thomas Mann's second novel was published: *Königliche Hoheit* (*Royal Highness*). It tells the story of a prince of a small state who, facing financial ruin, meets the daughter of an American billionaire. Their marriage is one of convenience, but eventually they find *'ein strenges Glück'* ("an austere happiness"). The novel can be interpreted as the novelization of Thomas's courtship of and marriage to the fabulously wealthy Katia.

In 1911, after an aborted holiday on the Adriatic coast near Pula, Thomas Mann spent the summer in Venice, where he developed an obsession with a Polish boy called Władysław Moes, also known as Władzio. This homoerotic crush and other events that happened during his stay in the Hôtel des Bain on the Lido were the inspiration for his most famous novella, *Der Tod in Venedig* (*Death in Venice*), published in 1912. He had originally wanted to write a novella about Goethe at Marienbad, where the seventy-two-year-old giant of German literature fell in love with the seventeen-year-old Ulrike von Levetzov – even, through an intermediary, proposing to her.

The First World War led to a rift between Thomas and his brother Heinrich. The latter was against the war and had just finished *Der Untertan*, which was a satire of Wilhelmine Germany and banned after the outbreak of the war. Initially, Thomas had admired the novel, but when the war, in which neither brother served, broke out, he changed his mind. He celebrated the war, calling it a *Volkskrieg* ("people's war") which would lead to national cleansing and a cultural revival, an act of destruction but also of creation. He published his views on the war in 'Gedanken im Kriege' ("Thoughts in Wartime", 1914). Not long after that, he followed it up with an essay on Frederick the Great, defending the Prussian king's wars of aggression and thereby justifying Germany's invasion of Belgium. At the end of the war, he published his *Betrachtungen eines Unpolitischen* ("Reflections of a Non-Political Man", 1918), a book-length essay in defence of German *Kultur* (deep and traditional) as opposed to Western *Zivilisation* (shallow and progressive), framing the war as a culture clash, and attacking liberalism and literary figures like his brother who defend democratic principles.

In the chaotic aftermath of the war, Thomas Mann flirted ever so briefly with Communism, preferring that ideology to the victorious Western democratic powers. But when the Bavarian Soviet Republic was crushed by the German Army and the *Freikorps*, Thomas's sympathy was with the ensuing military dictatorship. In these years he also read and was impressed by Oswald Spengler's *Der Untergang des Abendlandes* (*The Decline of the West*, 1918 and 1922). But not long after that, he changed his political outlook and convictions and became a defender of the Weimar Republic and parliamentary democracy.

In the immediate years after the war his literary output steered clear of politics, and he published a novella about a man and his dog called *Herr und Hund* (*A Man and His Dog*, also known as *Bashan and I*, 1918) and a long poem about his youngest daughter when she was just a baby, *Gesang vom Kindchen* (*The Song of the Child: An Idyll*, 1919).

Between their marriage and the end of the First World War, Thomas and Katia had six children. Erika (1905–69), Klaus (1906–49), Golo (1909–94), Monika (1910–92), Elisabeth (1918–2002) and Michael (1919–77). Erika was a lesbian and became an actress, journalist and writer. She was very close to Klaus, and they often travelled together. In 1926 she married the actor Gustaf Gründgens, who was her brother's lover, divorcing him in 1929. In 1935 she contracted a marriage of convenience with W.H. Auden, who was a known homosexual, to get a British passport. Klaus was openly gay, and is best known for his novel *Mephisto*, based on his erstwhile lover Gründgens, who stayed in Nazi Germany to continue his career as an actor. Klaus committed suicide shortly after the Second World War. Thomas's son Golo was also gay, although much more private than his brother Klaus, and became a historian. Throughout her life, Thomas's daughter Monika felt unloved by her father. It is possible that she was seduced by one of her teachers when she was fourteen. When she travelled from Liverpool to Canada in 1940, her ship was torpedoed by a German submarine, and she spent fourteen hours in the water before being rescued. Her husband did not survive. Thomas Mann's daughter Elisabeth was the apple of her father's eye, and became a political scientist and international lawyer concerned with oceans and the environment. Michael became a musician and professor of literature.

Whether it was the strains and stresses of their marriage, their many children or the state of her lungs (it seems she was misdiagnosed with tuberculosis), Katia Mann regularly spent time in sanatoriums for long cures. From these she would send notes and comments on fellow patients to her husband. In 1912 Thomas Mann visited her in Davos and conceived of a novella, which grew into his most famous novel, *Der Zauberberg* (*The Magic Mountain*). In 1922 Thomas had met György Lukács, the Hungarian Marxist philosopher, who became the model for Naphta, the Jewish Jesuit and antipode of Settembrini, the proponent of the Enlightenment. These two characters engage in lengthy philosophical arguments in the novel. He had also met Gerhard Hauptmann, the famous German author and Nobel laureate (1912), who became the inspiration for Peeperkorn, the larger-than-life Dutch patient in the fictitious sanatorium, much to Hauptmann's chagrin. Despite his publisher's reservation about the length, the novel was published in 1924. It became an immediate success and was translated into many languages. By 1928, it had already been printed one hundred times.

In 1929 Thomas Mann was awarded the Nobel Prize for Literature. The Swedish committee has historically been rather conservative in its literary taste and has preferred serious, moral works over modern and experimental literature. It is probably for that reason that the committee singled out *Buddenbrooks*, despite the success of *The Magic Mountain*, and described Thomas Mann as "the German Tolstoy".

Two years before, in 1927, when he was fifty-two, Thomas had met the eighteen-year-old Klaus Heuser during a holiday on Sylt. He fell in love and invited the young man to his home in Munich, leading to jealousy from his son Golo.

In 1930 he published an autobiographical piece called *Lebensabriss* ("Brief Biographical Sketch"), not all of it entirely honest. 1930 is also the year in which he published *Mario und der Zauberer* (*Mario and the Magician*). The novella is often read as an allegory of Fascist Italy, which had fallen under the spell of a hypnotic conjurer. And still in the same year he held a speech in Berlin in which he acknowledged the economic crisis and the prevalent sceptical attitude towards parliamentary democracy, but stressed that the place of the German people was on the side of social democracy. The speech was disturbed by Nazis in the audience.

When Hitler had taken power and the Reichstag had been set on fire in early 1933, Thomas happened to be in Switzerland. He decided not to return to Germany. In the same year, he published the first novel of the tetralogy *Joseph und seine Brüder* (*Joseph and His Brothers*), an expansive and ambitious retelling of the Biblical story. The first novel is called *Die Geschichten Jaakobs* (*The Stories of Jacob*, 1933). It was followed by *Der junge Joseph* (*Young Joseph*, 1934), *Joseph in Ägypten* (*Joseph in Egypt*, 1936) and *Joseph der Ernährer* (*Joseph the Provider*, 1943). He considered these works to be his magnum opus.

In 1934 he travelled to the United States for the first time, eventually emigrating there in 1938 after the *Anschluss* (annexation of Austria). First he lived in New Jersey and taught at Princeton (1938–41). He was actively involved in anti-Nazi propaganda, and throughout the Second World War he recorded speeches aimed at German listeners. These were sent to London and broadcast in Germany. He also gave public lectures in defence of democracy and attacking Nazism. He met President Roosevelt, and in 1944 he became an American citizen. Until then, he had been travelling on a Czech passport, having been stripped of his German citizenship by the Nazis. By the time he became a US citizen, he had been living in Los Angeles since 1941, moving into a house he had built for himself and his family in the Pacific Palisades in 1942, now the Thomas Mann House.

While he was at Princeton, he published *Lotte in Weimar* (1939), in which Lotte, with whom Goethe's alter ego is in love in *The Sorrows of the Young Werther*, travels to Weimar to meet Goethe forty years afterwards. He also wrote 'Die vertauschten Köpfe' ("The Transposed Heads"), an adaptation of an Indian legend, published in Stockholm in 1940.

Three years later, whilst living in California, he published the last novel of his tetralogy about Joseph, followed a year later by 'Das Gesetz' ("The Tables of the Law", 1944), a reimagining of the story of Moses.

After the end of the Second World War he refused to return to Germany. In 1947 he published *Doktor Faustus: Das Leben des deutschen Tonsetzers Adrian Leverkühn, erzählt von einem Freunde* (*Doctor Faustus: The Life of the German Composer Adrian Leverkühn, as Told by a Friend*). In it, a modern composer sells his soul to the devil so that he can make highly wrought and complex music. The price he pays is that he is unable to love.

In 1951 Thomas Mann published *Der Erwählte* (*The Holy Sinner*), which takes as its inspiration the legendary story of Pope Gregory, who was born from incest and later unwittingly married his own mother. When he found out, he did penance by chaining himself to a rock. Eventually God sent a sign that he had been the chosen to become the next pope.

Thomas Mann returned to Europe in 1952 and settled in Kilchberg, Switzerland. In 1954 he published his last novel: *Die Bekenntnisse des Hochstaplers Felix Krull* (*Confessions of Felix Krull, Confidence Man*). It recounts the story of a charming impostor who succeeds in assuming the identity of an aristocrat. We never read about his downfall because the novel was not finished and only part one was published.

When on holiday in the Netherlands, shortly after his eightieth birthday, Thomas Mann was taken to hospital and wrongly diagnosed with thrombophlebitis (a blood clot in the vein of his leg). He was transported to Zürich, where the wrong diagnosis was confirmed. Not long afterwards, he died from a ruptured iliac artery aneurysm that led to severe internal bleeding. He died on 12th August 1955 and was buried in Kilchberg, in the same cemetery his wife Katia would be laid to rest in 1980.

EVERGREENS SERIES
Beautifully produced classics, affordably priced

Alma Classics is committed to making available a wide range of literature from around the globe. Most of the titles are enriched by an extensive critical apparatus, notes and extra reading material, as well as a selection of photographs. The texts are based on the most authoritative editions and edited using a fresh, accessible editorial approach. With an emphasis on production, editorial and typographical values, Alma Classics aspires to revitalize the whole experience of reading classics.

For our complete list and latest offers visit
almabooks.com/evergreens

ALMA CLASSICS

ALMA CLASSICS aims to publish mainstream and lesser-known European classics in an innovative and striking way, while employing the highest editorial and production standards. By way of a unique approach the range offers much more, both visually and textually, than readers have come to expect from contemporary classics publishing.

LATEST TITLES PUBLISHED BY ALMA CLASSICS

473. Sinclair Lewis, *Babbitt*
474. Edith Wharton, *The House of Mirth*
475. George Orwell, *Burmese Days*
476. Virginia Woolf, *The Voyage Out*
477. Charles Dickens, *Pictures from Italy*
478. Fyodor Dostoevsky, *Crime and Punishment*
479. Anton Chekhov, *Small Fry and Other Stories*
480. George Orwell, *Homage to Catalonia*
481. Carlo Collodi, *The Adventures of Pinocchio*
482. Virginia Woolf, *Between the Acts*
483. Alain Robbe-Grillet, *Last Year at Marienbad*
484. Charles Dickens, *The Pickwick Papers*
485. Wilkie Collins, *The Haunted Hotel*
486. Ivan Turgenev, *Parasha and Other Poems*
487. Arthur Conan Doyle, *His Last Bow*
488. Ivan Goncharov, *The Frigate Pallada*
489. Arthur Conan Doyle, *The Casebook of Sherlock Holmes*
490. Alexander Pushkin, *Lyrics Vol. 4*
491. Arthur Conan Doyle, *The Valley of Fear*
492. Gottfried Keller, *Green Henry*
493. Grimmelshausen, *Simplicius Simplicissimus*
494. Edgar Allan Poe, *The Raven and Other Poems*
495. Sinclair Lewis, *Main Street*
496. Prosper Mérimée, *Carmen*
497. D.H. Lawrence, *Women in Love*
498. Albert Maltz, *A Tale of One January*
499. George Orwell, *Coming Up for Air*
500. Anton Chekhov, *The Looking Glass and Other Stories*
501. Ivan Goncharov, *An Uncommon Story*
502. Paul Éluard, *Selected Poems*
503. Ivan Turgenev, *Memoirs of a Hunter*
504. Albert Maltz, *A Long Day in a Short Life*
505. Edith Wharton, *Ethan Frome*
506. Charles Dickens, *The Old Curiosity Shop*
507. Fyodor Dostoevsky, *The Village of Stepanchikovo*
508. George Orwell, *The Clergyman's Daughter*
509. Virginia Woolf, *The New Dress and Other Stories*
510. Ivan Goncharov, *A Serendipitous Error and Two Incidents at Sea*
511. Beatrix Potter, *Peter Rabbit*

www.almaclassics.com

Printed and bound by CPI Group (UK) Ltd, Croydon, CR0 4YY
06/02/2026
02048852-0003